Conscious & Subconscious: The Human Experience

Janey Marvin

Conscious & Subconscious: The Human Experience

Copyright © 2021 by Janey Marvin.

Paperback ISBN: 978-1-63812-046-9
Hardcover ISBN: 978-1-63812-048-3
Ebook ISBN: 978-1-63812-047-6

Published by Pen Culture Solutions   06/13/2021

Pen Culture Solutions
1-888-727-7204 (USA)
1-800-950-458 (Australia)
support@penculturesolutions.com

CONTENTS

CHAPTER 1

CONSCIOUS & SUBCONSCIOUS

LEARN THE FUNCTIONS OF THE CONSCIOUS AND SUBCONCSCIOUS.

THE WAY THEY CREATE YOUR IDENTITY:

The sameness of essential or generic character in different instances, all that constitutes the objective reality of a thing: Oneness. This distinguishes the character and personality of an individual. The element of our Identity is the multiplicand that leaves any element of the set to which it belongs unchanged when combined with it by a specified experience. Identity is the quantity whose effect is to leave the multiplicand unchanged, equaling one thing to another, regardless of what the other may be. This is the creation of our unique personal qualities. Your Identity means that regardless of your life circumstances or experience, you think, feel, and behave the same. Change is not a subconscious process. If you change, you must consciously choose to change, and work to change. You must change your thoughts, your feelings, and your behaviors regardless of change in your circumstances and experiences.

Your Identity is an Element of your whole being and the subconscious takes data from the sense of sound and sight to create your identity. So literally, what you have seen and what you have heard, in addition to your conscious response to the sensory data becomes your identity in a subconscious program/model. Identity is therefore also based upon your Past, for Past

1

is the first Element of Time and this is processed and stored in the data from the senses of sound and sight.

AND REALITY:

A quality or state of being real in any event, entity, or state of being; A totality of real things and events that are neither derivative nor dependent but exists necessarily; The totality of our state of actually existing in the real world, as we perceive it to be. Our reality is also a subconscious program/model and as such, creates our life experiences.

REALITY: Reality Is a Totality. It is a quality or state of being real, the totality of real things, and events. Any totality consists of 3 separate Elements and the following is a list of the Elements which create Reality:

1st Element) Space; A measurable period during which an action, process, or condition exists or continues; Non-spatial continuum that is measured in terms of events which exceed one another, from past, through present, to future. In essence, Time is merely a standard of measurement between events. The more events exceeding one another, the shorter the measurement of between the events. Time is linear, and dependent upon the events, time can seem dimensional.

2nd Element) Time; A period of time or it's duration a limited extent in 1, 2, or 3 dimensions, consisting of the Distance, Area and Volume set apart and available; A boundless 3-dimensional extent in which objects and events occur, and have relative position and direction, even beyond earth's atmosphere and solar system.

3rd Element) Matter; The substance of which a physical object is composed of, material substance which occupies space, has mass, and is composed predominantly of atoms consisting of protons, neutrons, and electrons that constitutes the observable universe, and that is interconvertible with energy. Matter is often a material substance of a particular kind, or for a particular purpose. Matter is the indeterminate subject of Reality; the Element in the universe that undergoes formation and alteration, a formless substratum of all things which exists only potentially, and upon which form acts to produce Realities.

WHAT THE SUBCONSCIOUS IS:

The part of the Brain that...

Processes and stores all Data.

Processes Data prior to conscious having access to any Data.

Stores and governs our Emotions.

Governs our Desires and Behaviors.

Governs Self Image and Self-Talk.

Governs all "Automatic" learning's and functions.

Governs and Stores all Memory.

The subjective part of the brain.

Thought does not just come to conscious as a first part of the brain process. All thought that comes into the conscious is processed by the subconscious, prior to conscious having any access to it. Any thought coming to the conscious must have been prior programmed (approved) by conscious, for it to even come from the subconscious. If conscious responds to thought with a counter (more positive) thought of even having or knowing the thought repetitively, the subconscious will no longer send the negative thoughts to conscious. What is responded to by the conscious part of the brain in a manner of not interested in, or not cared about, will eventually stop even coming up to the conscious. This is the reason there are some things in our life's experience we just don't notice.

The process of storing and governing all the different parts of the self creates the programs and models of what we experience as automatic thought, feeling, and behavior. These are all compiled from sensory data from our environment, along with our own conscious response to the data. The subconscious doesn't create this, it just processes and stores it all, until one day, there is enough data stored that it's a complete program file and is now functional.

WHAT THE CONSCIOUS IS:

The part of our Brain that…

1) Perceives.

2) Evaluates.

3) Judges.

4) Decides.

5) Perceives, Evaluates, Judges, and Decides about All Data coming from the Subconscious.

6) The Objective part of the Brain.

Conscious May Override the Subconscious Programs.

The fact that our conscious is the objective part of our brain makes it a very important part of the subconscious belief about the data. Some people may experience a same, or similar sensory experience, and the conscious response being different for different people, can make completely different programs from the same data. For example, if the light gets shut off and a child is in the dark, and the conscious response is of a negative nature, verses, a positive nature, and maybe even creative fun nature, the programs can vary even to a point of fear and apprehension, verses, confidence and wonder.

Conscious is not programmed on its ability to perceive, evaluate, judge, and decide. Even though, the data coming into conscious becomes programmed based upon conscious response. The way conscious can perceive, evaluate, judge, and decide about the data is always instantly changeable by conscious. It isn't always easy to perceive a same or similar thing differently. Though, it is very possible for conscious to do this. The subconscious programs cannot be changed. Though, new programs can be created by conscious practicing; perceiving, evaluating, judging, and deciding differently.

The perceiving ability in the conscious part of the brain is our ability to attain an awareness and understanding of what our senses are processing. This is an observing process where we may discern for ourselves to recognize and realize our experiences.

Evaluating is the conscious ability to determine the value or significance of our sensory experiences. This ability of evaluating is the process conscious uses to determine the characteristics and merits of our experiences.

Judging is the conscious ability to form an opinion about the experience through careful weighing of evidence and testing of premises which we determine significant. Judging is consciously determined after inquiry and deliberation, and after testing evidence conscious has perceived.

Deciding is the conscious ability to make a final choice and select a course of action, based upon the conclusion of the data and process. This becomes an infinitive conclusion and brings the conscious process to a definitive end. This is the ability of our Choice and our Free Agency. This comes because of our choice to live. Once the Deciding process is complete, any previous consideration of the matter, any cause for doubt, debate, or wavering controversy, is very difficult to achieve.

All of this conscious "processed data" is sent immediately back to the subconscious, where this data is processed the exact same way all other data is processed in the subconscious. This conscious "feedback" to the subconscious about the data is the controlling factor of the way the data is to be defined, programmed, and modeled for the rest of our lives.

No wonder change is so hard. No wonder human beings debate and won't even consider another's opinion after they are programmed. This is a subconscious function, to take the data in and process the data and create our Identity, our Reality, and every aspect of our being from this data. Conscious defines and makes the final conclusive ending determination about the data, and then, we are that way all our lives.

Remember though, conscious can, and does override subconscious about the data. And if we understand the way the brains work, could we not learn to work them ourselves? Of course, we can. Sales people do this all the time. Some people come by it naturally, some are trained in it, and others can take charge of our brains. Nonetheless, we can also learn to direct and take charge of our own mind.

HOW DOES SUBCONSCIOUS PROCESS DATA

1st) Absolute Truth and Reverse Effect (truths opposite).
2nd) Major and Minor Meta Programs (Data compression).
3rd) Physics Laws of 1) Correspondence, 2) Similarity, 3) Unity.
4th) Sensory Firing Orders.

Being the subjective part of the brain, every micro bit of data from the environment is accepted as absolute truth by the subconscious, so there is a part of the processing that creates an opposite for each bit of data coming in. Subconscious is not perceiving, nor deciding anything. It is merely processing and storing all the data. The Reverse Effect assures that the data for the conscious to process, is not limited, but, open to any decisions conscious decides about it. This process gives us choice. It guarantees that any data and programs in the subconscious has a complete opposite file waiting to be accessed by the subconscious for conscious. If, and when, conscious "changes its mind" to think, perceive, and decide differently. This reverse effect process gives us the ability to truly know the solution whenever we are consciously aware of the problem. To be able to have the answer when we are consciously aware of the question. To be capable of perceiving, evaluating, judging, and deciding from opposite perspectives whenever conscious decides to access these program model files. Every micro bit of data in the subconscious has a complete equal amount of opposite data processed, just the same way the real data was processed, filed, and programmed to the same degree. The scripture, "There must needs be opposition in all things" is an actual process used by our brains to gather and store all the information ever received by the human brain.

There are many "meta-programs" the subconscious uses to compress all the data, to be able to fit it into files. Even though a small portion of the brain is used in a life time, Albert Einstein used 10% of his brain mass. It takes massive compilations of data, memory, and conscious response for the data in one file to become a program model of our automatic responses. Meta-programs are "Major and Minor" for data compression for storage in the program files. Conscious can still access the data, even though the subconscious meta-programs will change the data for storage purposes. I go into these specifically throughout this book because these meta-programs do effect our conscious experiences temporarily.

The Physics of Correspondence is the determining factor for the way the meta-programs decide the different files to place the data in along with a conscious response. This is based upon similar data and similar conscious response. The subconscious will even shift some of the data to get it to be similar sensory for filing it. The files have to be open to simple similarities to accept its data. Correspondence is vital for the data processing, storage, and for the programs and models to function together properly.

Correspondence is the process whereby all things communicate with one another. This also refers to the process by which all things come into agreement with one another. In order for anything to interact or relate between anything else; (whether a member of an organized set already associated to other members or non-members not associated) everything must be able to correspond with other things or there is no interaction between the things. Even cells of our body correspond to other cells in the body. Correspondence involves sharing features back and forth, sometimes between dissimilar things. Meta-programs work to change the sensory data to make the different data's more similar, so it can be placed in an organized program with similar data. Sometimes data that comes in is not similar to any of the data already processed and stored in a program model file. This data is called "deviating" data. Deviating data is very dissimilar from other data and the similar data compression programs cannot change this data enough to get it to relate to the other data. Deviating data requires that both major and minor meta-programs go to work on existing program files and check for any data that can still be changed some, while remaining similar enough to stay in the program. The deviating data requires the Unity Principle of Correspondence to come into effect and delete micro data elements, or insert micro data elements, or even, completely rearrange the micro data elements of the deviating data, as well as data already in programmed files. This principle of Unity must "Transform" the data in order to make the deviating data more similar, so it also corresponds with the other data. This process has numerous effects on our conscious experiences. For example, oftentimes the deviating data, is data our dreams are made of until the data can correspond with other data and be stored. Deviating data free floats throughout our neurology until it is unified to fit more similar with other data. If a compilation of deviating data adds up, especially from a traumatic event and will not change no matter what the data compression programs do, the subconscious will take other data from other files and deviate it, to create a past memory and create future memories of the traumatic deviating data.

If the data isn't able to correspond together in the file, the file can malfunction, and the conscious effect of this can be to think, feel, or behave very differently and not know why. Maybe even feel like we aren't our self anymore. If the different files can't correspond with each other, then we are running on half of what we are used to or capable of.

The sensory data firing sequence is completely dependent on the sense that is fired first in the subconscious. Depending on the first sense fired, there is a specific sequential firing order the central nervous system fires through the other sensory data program files. Because data from each sense is used to create different programs in the subconscious, each different sensory firing order or sequence creates different types of personalities with different natural strengths and weaknesses. This is detailed extensively in my books on Holographic Human Transformation Theory. Though,

I do detail some as it pertains to subconscious function and conscious consequences.

WHAT DATA DOES THE SUBCONSCIOUS PROCESS

Most of the Data the Subconscious Processes is Sensory Data from the environment:

Memory; 50%

Symbols; 50%

Memory comes in a variety of disguises and again the conscious response becomes an actual part of the memory. Genetic memory is a memory we don't talk so much about. Though it is just as real in our brain as is our memory from our personal life experiences. Genetic memory is just event memory; it doesn't include the conscious response to the event. Genetic memory is more difficult to recognize because it's a program model without the conscious response programmed into it. So, it may take a few times of perceiving it to be aware, before we make our own decisions and judgements about it. A good thing to do with Genetic memory is to talk to family members or research ancestry and put your own conscious perceptions, evaluations, judgments, and decisions in about the event. We already know some of our ancestry. Some is good, and sometimes, it is of a negative nature. Regardless, of the positive or negative, decide for yourself the conscious response to ancestral events.

HOW THE SUBCONSCIOUS STORES DATA

Data is stored in the Subconscious after it is processed into Models and Programs throughout different areas of our Brain and our Neurology. This stored data becomes programmed responses based upon conscious response to the repeated data. Once the data is compiled with enough conscious instruction, it becomes the programs, we consider to be ourselves.

Different sensory data is stored in different areas of the brain and different programs are created based upon the different sensory information. Different sensory data is used to create different kinds of programs and responses. Sound and sight data is used to create our mental processes, our identity, and our personality. Touch and energy data is used to create our emotional responses, our relationships, and our actions and intuitions. Taste and smell data is used to create our behavioral response programs, our beliefs about character, and our beliefs about strategies. There are many other programs and aspects created just based upon our sensory data, and our conscious responses to the data when it comes to conscious.

Sensory data itself is stored and accessed based upon similarity of data, and similarity of programming the data is used for. This data is stored in different areas of the brain for easy access and it is accessible through the central nervous system throughout our brain. Also, through the rest of our body. Just behind each human eye is over 360,000 nerve endings that go to the brain and other areas of our being. So even though data is stored as programs and models of our being, it can be accessed throughout our being through our central nervous system. So, we have pressure points and different areas where massaging the area can bring up different thoughts, feelings, and behaviors. It can bring up memories and all aspects of the programs compiled in the subconscious which make us human.

Data from the different Senses are stored and accessed through out our Neurology in Separate areas of our body.

Not only is data and programs stored in the brain, there are different neurological pathways the different programs are firing along throughout the entire body. It is also important that these neuro-paths remain unblocked for the programs to function properly. Neurological blocks can happen because of muscle stress and tension, injury, anything from a mental thought, an emotional problem, or physical can cause the neuro-pathways to block. When these pathways are blocked, the sensory programs might not be able to be accessed. This can in turn cause our conscious to have stress, be confused, anxious, other hard to manage states of mind or emotions, and physical stress.

Emotional Data is stored based on Similarity of Chemicals not Events. The limbic system creates the different chemicals not only for our organs and other body systems, also for our emotions. These emotional responses also become programmed responses and a chemical is released from the limbic system whenever sensory stimuli associated with the emotion is accessed. The central nervous system has receptor sites along its neuro-paths that receive these chemicals based upon the receptor site code for receiving the chemical and the chemical code coming along the neuro-paths. Along the central nervous systems pathway are dendrites and chemicals. Emotional responses become encoded on these parts of the neuro-paths. Any nervous system firing through the dendrite can trigger the emotional response with no sensory stimuli triggering the response.

Emotions are chemically based and just as the Meta-programs store the sensory data based upon similar frequency of the sensory data, emotion is stored on similarity of chemical.

There are different maps showing the different areas of the brain and programs and function in the areas. There are maps of the central nervous system throughout the human body and the areas of the brain and the central nervous system maps correspond together for each human being.

CONSCIOUS CAN OVERRIDE THE SUBCONSCIOUS

Because of Reverse Effect in the way the Subconscious Processes Data, Conscious has Choice about all the Programs, Models, Beliefs, and Data in the Subconscious.

I have spoken of the importance of the conscious response to anything we are consciously aware of. I have talked of using the objective ability of conscious to perceive conscious thought differently than the way you have in the past. Some of the things we might be consciously aware of are thought, feeling, behavior, self-talk, self-identity, world-view, linguistics (the words we use to express our thought, feeling, and describe our behavior), life patterns in relationships, goals, and choices. Conscious may seem like a small part of our brain mass and though it doesn't store the data and programs, it is still the most important part of all our environment feedback and program creations. Conscious decides what the data from the environment is going to mean and the way it will affect us for the rest of our lives. Conscious can change meanings of our past, programs in our present, and open pathways for our future. Conscious has choice. Even though the conscious is only receiving 5, 7, or 9 whole bits of data from the subconscious every .22 of a second, this becomes 1,469 whole bits every minute of our life. A whole bit is a complete list of all the data regarding any given stimuli or topic resulting in almost 1,500 complete files every 60 seconds. Conscious is aware of this information and evaluates, judges, and decides everything about it. The subconscious is not even aware of what the data is. Conscious makes the decision about what it is, and what all it means, and the ways of using or not using it. The trick is in getting the conscious to perceive, evaluate, judge, and decide Differently about the data. Conscious is completely capable of doing all of this differently. Though, most human beings are so stubborn we just refuse to do so. Conscious makes the final determination regarding any data and programs created and stored by the subconscious. Our Identity, Personality, Self-Image, Character Traits, Beliefs, any and every aspect we end up calling "self", is made from data from our environment and our conscious responses to that data.

With Reverse Effect, a thought of one thing automatically indicates an opposite or different thought. This is true for any of the subconscious program models. The fact that one thing exists means an opposite or different thing also must exist. So, our awareness of one choice naturally creates an awareness and choice of another.

HOW DOES SUBCONSCIOUS ACCESS THE DATA

1) Similar Sensory Input

2) Time

3) Conscious Focus

4) Specific Neurological Firing Orders (Sequence)

5) Subconscious is always processing Data

Through our central nervous system, the data is processed through neurological pathways to different areas of the brain and neurological pathways throughout the body. These pathways are created differently depending on the conscious responses to the various data. Correspondence effects this process based upon a similar input already existing in a program.

A change in conscious focus can cause the firing sequence to also change. This results in a difference in subconscious response that may actually be experienced on a conscious level. An example of this, is as simple as just consciously focusing on a word or phrase you naturally use and changing the word or phrase and having a very different emotional feeling. The phrase "I am" is an Identity level indicator. Simply being aware of when you use this, and then changing the "I am" to "I feel" can cause a subconscious change in neurological firing, resulting in a feeling and thought change. "I am a failure", verses "I feel like a failure", may decrease the feeling of failing. I recommend being very careful and consciously aware of when, and where, and how you even use the "I am" or "I'm" words, as they not only indicate a core belief, they can create new core beliefs.

DOES CONSCIOUS GET ALL THE DATA THE SUBCONSCIOUS HAS AND PROCESSES

Conscious must give Subconscious permission to give Conscious certain Data.

Conscious gets 5, 7, or 9 whole bits of Data every .22 of a second. Subconscious gets everything in its environment as well as what conscious responds to any data with. Subconscious can look at a page on a book and in less than a second can have every word on the page being processed by it. Speed reading is just a matter of allowing subconscious to do its job and conscious letting (allowing) it all to be perceived by conscious. Conscious can look at a tree and within less than a second, subconscious has already processed every leaf and branch of the tree. Conscious is the part of the brain that is limiting us, not the subconscious. When we experience limitations, it is a conscious directive.

All the data stored in the subconscious is available for conscious access, conscious decides what data it does, and does not choose to be aware of. These conscious decisions become subconscious programs and conscious has to go through a process of re-programming the subconscious to give conscious the data. The conscious process of re-programming the subconscious is quite simple; "repetition and compounding". The repetition is simply to repeat, repeat, repeat, and the compounding is to do the repetitions with breaks or distraction in-between over a period of time. This is the same way we all became programmed in the first place.

As innocent children our conscious may be filled with wild imaginations that come with emotional responses. Once the program models are created in the subconscious these begin to diminish in our conscious mind. In other words, we may consciously forget them. We become more concerned with our environment and the responses others in our life have to events in our environment. By the time we are about 8 years old, many of our program models we will live with for the rest of our lives are created. The subconscious at this point can only give conscious access to the program models conscious has given it permission to let it be aware of. These program models obviously are not all positive programs. Still, the conscious has supported these program models and agreed to them. You cannot receive data from your subconscious that your conscious mind has not agreed to accept.

The 5, 7, and 9 different amounts of data coming into the conscious every .22 of a second can be dependent on levels of stress or emotional state. An individual's emotional state of being. Especially, if they are on medications that effect these, can also determine the amount of data that will come into the conscious. The greater stress or harmful state of being, the less conscious access. The better state of being, the more conscious access. Being able to emotionally deal with life's experiences, meditation, or other exercise of conscious focus can increase the data to 9 or a higher level.

Altered States of Conscious determine the number of times per second that Conscious Processes the Data; The conscious perceiving, evaluating, judging, and deciding the data objectively. The less times per .22 of a second the data is consciously processed, the more the conscious is aware of in the data. The more times the conscious processes the data, the less conscious actually is aware of in the data. Conscious perceives, evaluated, judges, and decides the data coming into it from the subconscious from between 20, to less than 4 times every second. So, the less times per second the data is processed, the more of the data the conscious can understand. The amount of data per second is not changing. Only the cycles per second of how fast the conscious will process the data is changed. This helps to explain the feelings of anxious and overwhelmed and other stressful responses a person may be consciously aware of. The conscious is processing (perceiving, evaluating, judging, and deciding) 2,938 whole bits of data at 1,200 times per minute, might cause some states of distress. An Alpha state of conscious cycles per second of 7-14, would range from 420 to 840 times per minute of the same 2,938 whole bits of data. A Theta Level of conscious ranges from 4 to 7 times per minute of perceiving, evaluating, judging, and deciding the 2,938 whole bits of data. This calculates to 2,938 whole bits consciously processed 240 times per minute. On a Delta (sleep) level, the conscious is still processing the same amount of data less than the 240 times per minute. Subconscious does not alter in its structures, patterns, and processes. Only conscious states and nature is changeable.

FUNCTIONS OF THE LIMBIC SYSTEM

The Limbic System is located between the right and left hemispheres of the brain. It is referred to as the Chemical part of the Brain. It is also referred to as the Reptile Brain. This is the part of the brain where the fight or flight and other natural responses are that we are born with. We are born with the fear of falling and the fear of loud noises. From this, we have an automatic response referred to as the startle reflex. All other fears just as other emotional responses are created and programmed by our conscious response to data. This can also be programmed by our conscious responses to life's experiences. Our conscious perceptions and decisions about our life experience is what determines even our feelings (emotions) about the experience. All of our emotions come from the Limbic System and is coded through the central nervous systems into receptor sights located along the central nervous system.

WHAT ROLE DOES THE LIMBIC SYSTEM HAVE ON OUR CONSCIOUS EXPERIENCE

Different Sensory Stimuli responds based upon our Conscious thought response to the Sensory stimuli. When we have emotion, this releases different brain (Limbic) chemical. These Chemicals store on Similarity of Chemical not sensory stimuli. Emotion governs our strength of desire and governs our behaviors, emotions are programmed, chemical compositions. Decide what it is you desire and what behaviors needed to have your desires, consciously govern your emotions to create your desire. The chemical structure of the emotion is encoded on the dendrite of the central nervous system and remains there for an extended period of time and similar chemical structure stores together.

When emotion is added to our self-talk, meditation or other practices, the chemical composition of the emotions is encoded on the brain wave thought pattern. Just as the brain wave itself goes beyond Wi-Fi capability, the emotion encoded in the wave always goes with it.

CREATIVE SUBCONSCIOUS

When Sensory stimuli is Data Processed in the Subconscious without finding a similar program to place it in and it cannot be unified with any other data, the Creative Subconscious will take the Data and actually Create a Past and Future for the Data. The Creative Subconscious is also the part of the brain that is involved with processing similar and deviating data storage. If similar sensory data cannot be found to file, the data in this part of the brain will create a whole new file for the data. It will go so far as to create a past and a future for the data that has no other similar data in any of our already existing files. So, a traumatic experience with no other similar data can result in past and future memories of the data as created by this part of the brain.

This may help explain violent crime victim's responses of feeling guilty for the crime committed against them. The event having a created past leading up to it, and a created future of the event, all created by the brain. This may help explain PTSD and other such traumatic events people have experienced and their future fears of the event.

WHAT WAYS DOES THE SUBCONSCIOUS PROCESS THE DATA FOR CONSCIOUS

The Subconscious consists of Major and Minor Meta-Programs, which are the Filtering Process Systems the different Sensory Data is Processed through. These are also referred to as Data Compression programs.

Every aspect, function, and element of being human is filtered through the data compression programs and they all inter-relate with one another. Major data compression programs relate to associated senses in the subconscious. Associated senses are: Sound and Sight, Touch and Energy, Taste and Smell. Minor data compression programs are related to individual senses.

EXAMPLES OF MAJOR META PROGRAM PROCESSING FILTERS

Sound and Sight: Deletes; remove from the experience by erasing, backspacing, creating a blank space.

Touch and Energy: Distorts; twist out of true meaning or proportion, change the natural, normal state and represent falsely.

Taste and Smell: Generalizes; derive or induce a general conception or principle from particulars and draw a general conclusion or give a general applicability and make things indefinite.

EXAMPLES OF MINOR META PROGRAM PROCESSING FILTERS

Sound: Deletes by Sameness.

This is the reason the conscious awareness of a same sound dissipates after a period of time. Just like the ticking of a clock.

Sight: Deletes by Difference.

This is the reason conscious awareness of something to "see" isn't always noticed at first. Get a different vehicle and notice all the similar vehicles around.

Touch: Distorts by Amplification.

This is the reason of a lot of touch sensations increased to a point of chills and goosebumps and feeling its effects in other areas of the body.

Energy: Distorts by Diminishing.

This is the reason many people struggle with their own actions, intuitions and confidence.

Taste: Generalizes by Sameness.

This is the reason most people have food preferences.

Smell: Generalizes by Difference.

This is the reason smell may be noticed that are different and conscious can relate it to another experience quickly.

HOLOGRAPHIC LEVELS

Character and Strategy

Relationship and Action

Values and Ideas

Spiritual

Holographic Levels are easily identified by the words a person uses to express or communicate. Even words in their conscious thought. Words pertaining to, or referencing the different levels, indicate that level of programming in the subconscious. The key to these levels, is in knowing that something cannot be fixed on the level the problem exists on. You must go to the next level at least, to fix the level the problem is on. For example, you cannot fix the character or strategies, except the person relates and acts differently. Character and strategy came from relationship and action. You cannot change relationship and action, except to change your values and ideas. You cannot change values and ideas except to change the spiritual. Just knowing this may help save a lot of time and trial and error in helping yourself or another person.

CENTRAL NERVOUS SYSTEM

Synapse

Dendrites

Receptor Sights

Each human body contains enough nerve in their nervous system to go around the earth and out to Jupiter and back several times (A lot of nerve). The synapse is the space between each section of nerve. The dendrite are the junctions where the neuro-path of the nervous system can branch off into different directions. Receptor sights are located throughout the central nervous system and receive the chemical to add emotion to the programs and data.

LINGUISTICS

Neuro fire: Words are not just stored in one file in the human brain, they are stored based upon similarity of frequency, tonality, sensory reference, and different element indicators. We do not consciously put our thoughts, nor our expressed words together in the conscious mind prior to thinking, nor expressing them. The words for both our thought and our verbal expressions are collected through the specific neuro-paths the words are stored in subconsciously. Remember, or go back and refer to the speed at which the conscious and subconscious work together. Just a sensory stimuli, an emotion, and intuition gets a response from the subconscious. Within .22 of a second the subconscious puts the data together for conscious access. Based upon this neuro-fire and the words conscious has to think or express it, the pathways can be identified. This neuro-pathway also has an opposite based upon reverse effect. And again, if you have the question, you also have the answer. If you have the problem, you have the solution. If you have the weakness, you have the strength. Learning the functions, programs, and nature of the senses, you can identify the answers, the solutions, and the strengths yourself.

Definitions and use of words: Such as…

Weave Words: These are very simple words and they have a powerful effect on the subconscious. These words cause the subconscious to take whatever is said in the first of a sentence and weave, glue, and add it to whatever is said at the end of the sentence. As I have read the scriptures, these little words are used often by Jesus Christ in His speaking. Examples of these words: Still, while, as, and, even though, also, again. There are other words able to have this same of similar effect on the subconscious. Any word that is a synonym to any of these words would work.

What using these words does, is to take the first of a sentence, such as: "Life has been hard for me…." Still" …. "I go on believing I can win."

Please write other sentences and use these glue words in between the first and last of the sentence. Have the first of the sentence be the more negative part, then the glue word and then the positive part to end the sentence. Also scale out how you feel about just the negative from 0 to 10, then do the sentence with the glue word and a positive end and scale your feeling about the sentence again from 0 to 10.

Addictive Words: "Need" indicates a lack of something requisite, desirable, or useful. Something which is a physiological or psychological requirement for the well-being of an organism. "Need" can indicate even to a state of poverty. "Want" also indicates being needy or destitute, to have or to feel need all indicate a lack of. "Have to have" is a state of lacking and in great need of.

These three words are referred to as addictive words as they all indicate a subconscious program/model that is programmed for lacking. Often times these words are referenced in sentences with the other words actually tied to a programmed core belief. Core belief programs either help us attain our goals and desires or keep us from attaining the very things in our life we desire yet struggle attaining or acquiring.

Whenever you use any of these words in a sentence please notice the sentence and consider changing the words: Want, Need, or Have to Have, for words or phrases such as: I am working on...., I will acquire...., I seek....

Examples of sentences containing the addictive words indicating programs to have a lack: "I want peace in my life", "I need to have you understand what I'm saying", "I have to have success at what I'm doing." Want, need, or have to have, used in these ways indicate a program modeled to not attain whatever it is that is wanted, needed or have to have. When you hear yourself using the addictive words, notice what it is that you do want, need, or have to have, and whatever it is, it is something you are programmed to lack. Being programmed to lack indicates that you will never get it because you are programmed to not have it.

Replacing the addictive words in the sentence with words like desire, working for, intending to achieve, and other similar examples can make a great difference. Changing the words repetitively over a period of time can create a program for success, as opposed to the lack of program. Examples of replacing addictive words with other phrases in a sentence: "I desire peace in my life. I am working at having you understand what I'm saying. I intend to have success at what I'm doing."

Simply removing these addictive words from your language can make a great difference in the way you feel and your life experience. The words we use play a great role in our life experience. If you'd like to get a little more complicated in your use of the addictive words, you can use them in sentences (on purpose) where you do not want something. Using the addictive words when you would prefer to lack in something also has a lacking effect in the subconscious. Some examples of this might be: "I want to go to bed and feel wide awake." "I need to study this book harder to understand it." I have to have the cold and flu you have."

Major and Minor Meta Words:

Some Major Data Compression Programs are:

Delete: words indicating delete would be: zero, erase, cut, end, home, return, space, not.

Distort; contort, falsify, most words beginning with mis-shape, misunderstand, mistake.

Generalize; words indicating generalizations are any, all, always, every, never.

Examples of generalization statements: "I never seem to be happy or make the right choice." "Everyone always treats me like I'm nobody." These indicate your own core belief programs.

Minor Meta-Programs are sameness, difference, amplify, and diminish. Any words indicating these also indicate the sense the Meta-program is used in.

Time reference:

Time consists of: Past, Present, and Future. Words indicating these different time frames indicate subconscious programs of the time references of the topics of the sentence the time reference word is used with. Past: had, was, did, didn't, done, can't, knew, that: Present: has, am, is, do, have, know, this. Future: will, may, won't, could, would.

If words indicating the Past are used in a sentence indicating the present, then the topic referred to not present, it is past. Example: "I was happy now" verses "I am happy now." Words indicating the future used in a sentence referencing the past, means it is not future referenced, only past referenced. "Tomorrow I had it figured out." "I know it was done later."

Whatever the examples are, the fact is to be aware of the time reference words you are actually using, as compared to the subjects and topics you might think you are referencing about. For many of us our past just projects into our future, so our future never changes, it only repeats our past. Our present is stuck in our past and the easiest way of recognizing these programs is by noticing any references of time in our sentences. When you become aware of the time reference you are actually using, just simply change the time reference, to the time you prefer it to be, and repeat the sentence. Just doing this repetitively will also help create new and better program models in your subconscious and change your life experience and the way you emotional respond to it.

Sensory Reference:

Even though, all the human senses can do the other senses, they still have their separate program/models, functions, elements, and individual aspects. There are words that indicate the different senses information is coming from, and these then indicate the different program/models and their individual functions.

Sight: See, saw, look, perceive, view. Sound: hear, heard, talk, tell. Touch: soft, rough, any texture reference words. Energy: high, low, ecstatic, radiant. Taste: Bitter, sweet, sour, salty. Smell: Roses, rain, perfume, any descriptions of the way something smells.

Words indicating the different senses also indicate that senses individual functions and aspects.

Literal, figurative, and symbolic meanings and applications of words:

My years of research for my books has had a large focus on the words themselves and their meanings. Each word has been taken first literally in its exact meaning and each word's literal meaning written together in a dialogue. Then that dialogue has been written to a figurative meaning from the literal. Last but not least, many of the techniques I have developed is the symbolic meaning or representations of the literal and figurative dialogues. To me, I say it has all just been that simple. Even though, the compilation of all the written material has been years in the making.

Literal means adhering to the facts to the ordinary construction and primary meaning of a term or expression. Literal lacks any imaginative or exaggeration or embellishment of any of the facts. It is free of anything not actual.

Figurative: Is just a representation or a resemblance of the real thing. Expressing something in terms normally denoting another with which it may be regarded as analogous, (metaphorical). Figurative is non-literal.

Symbolic: Is just the way something might relate or be characterized by something else.

Many things in life have different ways of applying them and interpreting them. This is true also of words. I have actually had a lot of awakenings taking words from a literal basis. Remember it's the conscious brain that is objective and is aware and able to evaluate and decide, not the subconscious.

Organ Language; Organ Language is simply words used in our thoughts and sentences indicating different body organs and/or that organs function. These words, when used on a conscious level are indicators and directives to organs and their functions. Be aware of when you use these words and the organs they reference and when you notice you use them change the usage and perhaps be more aware of the organ function. There are numerous examples of organ language and the effect it can have on the human body.

Phrases such as: "Give me a heart attack." "Chaps my ass". "Makes me sick to my stomach." "Takes my breath away". All of these seemingly simple phrases have an absolute effect on the subconscious, which then in turn, runs these organs and their functions.

Tonality: The arrangement or interrelation of the tones of words used in the sentences we express. The tone difference in our verbal expressions can indicate either a truth or a lie and a belief or a doubt depending upon the tone going up or down. If for example someone says, "I love you." And the tone goes to a higher pitch on the word "love or you", then it indicates that they don't love you or at least they question whether they do or not. If someone says, "I love you" and the tones all go down at the end of the word(s), this indicates they do love you and do not doubt that they do.

Become more aware of the tone of your voice as you speak your words, even though you might not had been consciously aware of this and other simple aspects before reading this, all of these differences come from the subconscious programs. Even listening to your tones as you speak and you might be speaking of not knowing a choice or a fact, just listening to your own voice tone can give you the subconscious information. Whether something is the best choice and whether something is the fact or not is even expressed in the natural tone with the words being expressed. Again, we do know so much more than we knew that we knew we just didn't know how to get to know it, these are ways of getting to know what we didn't know that we knew.

Bothers

JANEY MARVIN

The word bothers indicates both and so to express about anything that "bothers" you, only indicates that you have this same thing within yourself. "People not listening to others before they speak bothers me." Indicates that you do not listen to others before you just go ahead and speak, and this also bothers you. Other examples: "How rude they are really bothers me." Any time you use the word bothers indicates you do the same thing.

We cannot actually even see in another what isn't in ourselves.

Be aware of when you use the word "bother" and realize you have the same trait. I believe if we knew our problems, we would work to overcome them. So often the hardest part of overcoming a problem or a weakness is even realizing what it is and that we have it.

Learn the functions of the Conscious and Subconscious and the way they create your Identity and Reality. Use this book as a manual of getting to know yourself and others and begin to understand yourself and others. All of our program/models are just created from the data in our environment and our own conscious response to the data. You can create new program/models the same way the current ones were created, Repetition and Compound. Repetition and Compound is just repeating a thought, feeling, or action then compound it by doing something different then repeat it again. Repeat and Compound a desired program/model 5, 7, or 9 times and it will begin to do itself some. Keep your focus on enforcing the new program with continued repeating and compounding. This is the way our programs are created.

Learn the Language Patterns of True Success and Joy.

Simple, effective words and patterns of using these to attain your goals in life and help others. Words you should, could be using in your thoughts and your verbal expressions can make a complete change in the ways you think, feel, and respond. The main way we think is in our words, and the words in our own thought processes. Self-talk play a large role in our success. Just practice with the words I have written about in this chapter; keep a journal of the words you use, and don't use. Journal about the words and phrases you have changed and write about the different thoughts and feelings you might experience doing this. There are many more words that can help you have a happier life experience and there are different techniques in how to use words for more subconscious effects.

Linguistics: Identify and change your Core Beliefs through the words you use. I am statements indicate core belief. Be very aware of when you use any I am or I'm statements. I'm angry. I'm stupid. I'm hopeless. I'm upset. I'm done. I'm an addict. I'm an idiot. Whether these I am statements are verbalized or just thoughts, makes no difference. Either way, they have a great effect on the subconscious. Also, they indicate a core belief.

I am statements such as: I am great. I am happy. I am a recovering addict, alcoholic. I am successful. I am ready for life. I am able to deal with life. I am up to the challenge. I am grateful I am human. These I am statements are beneficial even if it takes conscious effort to do these at first. I am statements will still have a positive effect on you and your programs.

Holographic Levels: a simple pattern of our Inner Beliefs and aspects of our being stored deeply in the Subconscious. Easily Identified through simple word usage. Each of the different human senses create different parts of our whole being. Data from the different sense each has its own function as well as Major and Minor Meta-program processing the data. Every aspect of our being and every detail of our life relates literally, figuratively, or symbolically with one or more of our human senses. Getting to know this information and practicing and implementing the information and processes can help you get to know yourself and create aspects and beliefs to help you accomplish anything you choose to accomplish with your life.

Time: Learn the Totality of Time to change your Perception and Learn from your Past. You have been creating your Future all your life. There are of course three different Elements of Time: Past, Present and Future. Each element has its own function and its own patterns and processes. Man, sometimes teaches that you cannot change your past. The fact of the matter is we get our life's direction from the past. All reality is, anyway, is the way that we choose to perceive it. Our past is no different. All of life's experiences are a perception of the experience. We can, and in fact, we must practice changing our perception of the past, or our life's direction will never change. The future itself has a function of disorder. If the future was built upon order, then the future could never be any different than the past. Disorder is a fact of life and when disorder is experienced or perceived in our lives this is an indicator that the future can be rearranged. The future is the third element of time and the third element of transformation. Future being the third element of transformation means that all you need to do to adjust the disorder of the future, is to take whatever is available and rearrange or remodel it. Or, in more technical terms, permeate it. Time is a very significant aspect of our lives and time is mixed into every aspect of our being. Every organ, every program, every thought, feeling, behavior, has time built into it. It already has a past, a present, and a future. Time can be a difficult aspect to understand. Many of us have felt that time was against us; whether just not letting us go, or not coming into our lives right. Time serves an important function in our personality, our identity, and our beliefs. Time is as simple as any other aspect of our being. Past is stored in sound and sight, present is stored with touch and energy, and future is stored with taste and smell. Past, present, and future all have the functions, meta- programs, program/models, and elements of the senses they are programmed with. The only aspect of our time that we should be taking action on is our past, and the only action we should be taking for our past is to change our perception of the past. Present needs no action. Present is for our intuitions and our relations. Present is our emotion, and though many people do take action in the present on their relations and their intuitions and emotional, this oftentimes backfires on us. Future itself will work with the other two elements of time when we learn to let others take action, and our only process is to focus on rearranging our own beliefs and abilities to organize our future.

Time Model and its Linguistic Pattern: There is a language pattern to your speech which will help you Identify and control the effects of Time in your life's experience. Learn to create opportunities between your life's events, actions, and conditions. Practice the linguistics of proper time word use. Become more consciously aware of the way you verbalize, regarding time now. Keep a journal of this and learn to correct your words referencing proper time elements and journal about your experiences while doing this exercise.

The Gift: We all have Personality Overlaid imprints from our parents and society. There are traits and characteristics which just are not us. We have them to help another person change and grow. When the other person doesn't accept these, we continue to carry them ourselves. There are actually genetic memories in each of us from parents for many generations, this is true even if you are adopted. This genetic memory is passed on and includes society, cultural memory, and traits as well. Everyone comes to earth with something to be able to help someone else with also. Oftentimes, it takes another person pointing out to us our own weakness to get us to recognize and begin to change. Unfortunately, the way another points out our weaknesses to us, is by doing something that "bothers" us, or in some way, pushing our buttons. We all have experienced even a loved one, sometimes a family member, that triggers a negative or defensive, or some sort of programmed response in us that isn't good for our growth. It is these individuals and our responses to them that can indicate something to change in ourselves. Personality overlays from our parents can include their parents and so on. We all have characteristics and even physical traits from family. These characteristics and traits are passed on from generation to generation. At some point, someone must overcome these negative characteristics to stop them from being passed on anymore. Sometimes, even if a generation has overcome them, they can still be in the genetic composition and triggered later on.

Thoughts, Feelings and Actions:

These and much more of you is stored in your subconscious.

A very small portion of the Data we receive from our environment actually comes first to our conscious mind.

Any Data coming to our conscious mind comes from our subconscious mind, where it has been filtered already through the brains Major and Minor Meta-Programs. Only 5, 7, or 9 whole bits of Data actually comes into the conscious mind every .22 of a second. Conscious Function regarding this Data from the subconscious is to 1) Perceive the Data, 2) Evaluate the Data, 3) Judge the Data, and 4) Decide about the Data. The information from this conscious process then goes back to the subconscious where this is then processes just as Data through the subconscious Meta-Programs.

The subconscious Meta-Programs are similar to Data Compression Programs of a computer. The subconscious then takes this Data and places it into Models and Programs which decide our automatic responses, our thoughts, our emotions, and our behaviors. Even the 5, 7, or 9 whole bits of Data coming into our conscious mind every .22 of a second is already decided based upon what Models and Programs we already have in our subconscious anyway. Wow. I grew up thinking, it was all just me and I just thought and felt and behaved the way I did because it was my Identity. No, this is not true. Our thoughts, our feelings, and our behaviors are Models and Programs created through our brains processes. All this being based upon; 1) the Data, Feedback, and Anomalies in our environment, 2) our conscious responses to the 5, 7, or 9 whole bits of the Data coming into the conscious, and 3) most of our Models and programs were completed by the age of 8 years old.

The Subconscious takes in every micro-bit of Data from the environment; it processes and stores all this Data as individual Data, not a compilation of sounds, sights, feelings, or events. Each micro-bit of Data is, in and of itself, separate from the other Data available. The Subconscious processes these micro-bits of Data based on different Functions of the brain and Physics Laws.

The Data in the Subconscious is limitless, anything and everything ever available in the environment and the response from our conscious mind is stored in the Subconscious mind.

Programs are based upon the environments we grew up in and the responses of the people in our environment.

Getting to know our self is often times a process of just "remembering" and not a discovery process. All the information you must have at any given time is already in your subconscious. The trick is getting it to come to conscious. Conscious is the part of the brain that told the subconscious to not let it be aware of the data. Conscious must in turn convince the subconscious that it is ready to receive the data now.

Understand, Control, Create, and Effect your own Subconscious. These and other things about you that could normally take a Life Time to change, may change in moments, days, weeks, or a few months. Know the structure, patterns, and processes by which the brains function. Become aware of the linguistics you use to think and express yourself. Change your words, realize your potential, understand that your identity, and personality. Even your beliefs are just programs created by your environment. Take charge and become all you have imagined becoming, imagine beyond your greatest potentials. Reach for the sky and (program/model) create it.

If you have thoughts, feelings, and actions that you don't like about you, they come from you. If they are repetitive, they come from the subconscious and you can create new programs with some simple processes that take just a few moments. If your thoughts, feelings, or actions that you don't like are not repetitive, they only happened once or twice in your up to now life time (so they are just flying by and happened to hit you once or twice) and you don't like them, then honestly, that's a whole other concept and is not necessarily coming from our own subconscious.

Let's say for example that there are certain things that others do, and you have a certain response to their doing these things. Let's say for example that your response is anger or depression, or some other type of feelings or thoughts that you don't enjoy. You would normally have a tendency to blame the others for your response. Well, the truth of the matter is that the response you have is your response. And it is not the other persons fault that you respond the way that you do. These are programmed responses in you. They are triggered by what the others are doing because their doings are programmed in your subconscious to trigger the program inside you. The majority of the programmed responses we have, inside us, we were not born with these. They are learned program responses.

There are a few responses that we as human beings are born with.

31

Regarding: Fear, We are born with two natural responses to fear and two things we are naturally fearful of. The two things we naturally fear are loud noises and falling. Our two natural responses we are born with about these two fears is to flinch and/or scream. Most of our responses to most stimuli's are based on our own thoughts and feelings that we decided to have and put together to think and act to different kinds of stimuli of our own accord.

Life can be hard enough with all the outside influences on us. Let alone, when our own thoughts, feelings, or actions are hurting us too. We can't change the outside, or the world. But we can change the inside, or us, (you). Perception, the way we perceive things is key to everything else in our lives. Many people praise attitude. Attitude comes from perception. Attitude is not everything. It is merely a result of our perception. Attitude is simply an expression. Attitude is approximately 50 dendrite neuro-firing in our subconscious in the same micro second. The dendrite is similar to a junction in the central nervous system, where that section of the nerve can break off into many different directions. Often times the chemical which creates our different emotions builds up on the dendrite and we can actually experience emotion just by having the central nervous system fire through the dendrite. Attitude is identified in an infant by a smile, a frown, or other facial expressions they are not born with.

Perception is the way we perceive things. We perceive through our human senses. Each of our human senses has different meta-programs they go through in our subconscious prior to our conscious ever perceiving them. As human beings, we often perceive completely different things from the exact same sensory possibilities. Let alone, as humans, we may not even perceive, at all, certain sensory inputs of a situation that has sensory inputs available. Thus, we, as human beings, perceive differently. I say, for one, thank God, for this possibility and experience. Otherwise, we would all be the same, perceiving the same, attitudes, with the same human identities and personalities. In addition to our meta-programs, we have different sensory experiences that we don't enjoy or even might cause us discomfort or pain. Our conscious minds response to different sensory experiences, go as commands to our subconscious. So, if we think things such as, "I don't like that sound, feeling, or taste", and we think these kind of thoughts repetitively, our subconscious will stop letting our conscious mind know about that specific or similar sensory experience.

Our conscious responses to all things play a vital and often times seemingly permanent role in our reality of life. Every thought you have is considered a command to the subconscious and determines the way perception, judgment, and decisions are just automatically made about our life.

The thoughts, feelings, and doings that are from you, began many years ago. They are a part of you. The conscious mind can have thoughts so fast that it can be hard, at times, to figure out how to express them. Oftentimes, leaving us thinking we expressed everything we thought, as quickly as we thought it, but we didn't. Let alone, when there are unkind or hurtful things said to us. Listen to your conscious thought: Oftentimes, it is our own conscious thought saying unkind and hurtful things to us. Discouraging words from our own thoughts, are oftentimes more prevalent than others discouraging or hurtful words to us. Worry, stress, anger, depression, and whatever it is that you are experiencing is exacerbated by your own conscious mind. If you don't like these thoughts, or your own feelings, or your own doings, change them.

Elliot Aronson spent decades researching human behaviors. He is responsible for much of the information and the series of books called Social Animal. One of the researches in Social Animal is of positive verses negative comments expressed. To do the researches, there needs to be three separate groups studied: One group knows exactly what the research team is doing; another group doesn't even know a research is taking place; and another group is informed that the research is something very different than what it actually is. From this basis, the research team counted and tallied positive comments to children verses negative comments to children in various homes, and private and public schools in America. The highest percent of positive verses negative comments came from the first group which knew they were being researched for this and its tally was 20% positive to 80% negative.......

The human mind has been studied for decades; we know a lot today about the human mind. In the past, this information has been used in business to increase sales, collections, and other vitals of business. It's been used for intelligence work and investigating. Basically, in the past, this information was used for the whole and not available to the individual.

Motivational programs have incorporated this information into their programs. They aren't teaching you the functions of the brains, they have created techniques or processes based on the functions of the brain and you have to regularly pay to participate WITH them to get to the state of mind that they know how to take you to. You are often times paying them lots of money. Going to them helps make some corporation or company lots of money.

The conscious Functions of 1) Perceive, 2) Evaluate, 3) Judge, and 4) Decide, still is nothing more than what the subconscious Models and Programs are anyway. And, subconscious must have conscious permission to send any specific Data to the conscious prior to sending it to be processes. In addition, the conscious Functions experience of:

1) Perceiving; is our ability to attain an awareness and understanding of anything. Any and all things we are able to pick out and take in, to detect, discern, distinguish, notice, to become clear about the meaning of anything. There are other ways of saying this, still you don't even notice, let alone discern or be clear about anything that isn't already an Automatic- on-going subconscious Program or Model within you already. Sorry, you are not naturally, Open, nor wise, nor changeable, you are the representations of your own subconscious beliefs with your conscious responses added into them.

2) Evaluate; the ability to determine or fix the value, significance, worth, or condition of anything by careful appraisal and study. Your ability to assign a degree of value or worth, is another conscious Function though the Data it's getting is still based on pre-programs.

3) Judge; the ability to form an opinion about through careful weighing of evidence and testing of premises. The ability to Guess and Think, to come to a conclusion about anything. "Make up one's own mind."

4) Decide; the ability to make a final choice, to select a course of action, of an infinitive choice. Settle, Rule, Resolve, Fixing the Identity, character, scope or direction of something. Determining to do or not do a thing.

Conscious mind has allot of say in the subconscious pre-programs even though in order to consciously help the subconscious create New Models and Programs which can then be ran automatically by the subconscious:

1) The conscious must change its responses of understandings, discernments and things noticed in the Data the subconscious is sending.

2) The conscious must respond with different value, significance and worth of the Data it is already getting.

3) The conscious mind must form different and new opinions and weigh the evidence and testing by different premises.

4) The conscious mind must select new and different courses of action and infinite choice must become Open choice. Make up one's own mind in different and new ways with each amount of Data coming into it.

Just this change in the conscious response, conscious taking greater control over the same old subconscious Models and Programs, the subconscious will take these new responses and begin to create new Models and Programs based on greater conscious controlled response.

It's really just that simple and there are many different kinds of techniques and processes of assisting you in doing this.

When Hypnosis or Altered States of Conscious' is referred to, many people think of this as "messing with the subconscious". Reality of Hypnosis; Altered States of Conscious consists only of the cycles per second that the conscious processes the 5, 7, or 9 whole bits of Data it receives every .22 of a second. The subconscious Functions, Structures, Patterns, and Processes is not alterable. Subconscious is pre-programmed the same way in each and every person. Just as the heart, lungs, any other body Element or Organs are. There is no way known to man today, to alter the Total Functions, Structure, Patterns, and Processes of the subconscious. Knowing the ways, it does create Models and Programs can help the conscious take better control in creating new and managing the old Models and Programs.

In addition to Conscious' Functions, there are different levels of conscious; this simply refers to the cycles per second that the conscious repetitively goes through the Data from the subconscious to Perceive, Evaluate, Judge, and Decide about the Data. The lower the level of conscious cycles per second, the less numbers of times per second the conscious repeats through the Data for conscious to do its Function with the Data.

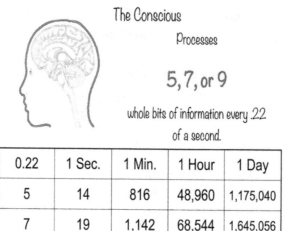

The Conscious

Processes

5, 7, or 9

whole bits of information every .22
of a second.

0.22	1 Sec.	1 Min.	1 Hour	1 Day
5	14	816	48,960	1,175,040
7	19	1,142	68,544	1,645,056
9	24	1,469	88,128	2,115,072

SUBCONSCIOUS

There is an actual Science of The Functions of the Brains.

The process of making the different programmed responses, processes of just doings, thinking patterns, and beliefs is quite simple. And once these different processes of being, and doing, are made or created, we just do and are, and be. Through a process called "Repetition and Compounding", we don't even need to consciously consider them anymore. We just, do and are and be. Then we just say things like, "Well, that's just me."

This is all good and well when we like these different programmed aspects of self, but when these programmed aspects of ourselves, are not helping us, or sometimes, even hurting us, it is in our, and oftentimes, others, best interest that we change these programmed aspects of ourselves.

Repetition is defined as a process of repeating a thing. To create or make a program in the subconscious, a thing just needs to be repeated. The repeat has to occur a certain number of times. Each of us may vary in the exact number of times repeated to have the subconscious just automatically do it for us without much conscious thought. In the beginning of each programmed process, we have to give a greater amount of time and thought to the programmed process which may become automatic from the subconscious after the process of Repetition and Compounding. Like anything, when we are first introduced to anything, at first, we have to maybe ask questions, study, and/or practice other ways of the Repetition process. Over a course of time with enough questions, answers, study, and/or practice, we can just do the thing and hardly have to even give much conscious thought to it, as we just can automatically do it. Oftentimes, even when we are doing something else at the same time. These are the kind of things we learn through Repetition and Compounding, that just become automatic programs run by our subconscious.

Compounding is another important aspect of getting anything to just become automatically ran by the subconscious without so much conscious thought. Sometimes, without any conscious thought, to a point that we could be doing the thing and not even consciously realize that we are doing the thing.

Compounding is basically the process of not Repeating for a space of time. Compounding can take place in different ways. Compounding can be processed simply by doing the Repetition process, then doing something else, and then going back to the Repetition process. So, when learning something new, ask some questions and get some answers, then go and do something completely different. Then go back and study the thing you're seeking to have automatically programmed, then go and do something completely different again. Then come back and practice the thing to automatically program, then go and do something completely different. Back and forth and back and forth. Kind of like how life ends up being anyway. This Compounding process of back and forth, and in and out of, and back and forth of the thing to be automatically programmed, and then leaving the thing to be programmed to focus conscious on another thing, and then back to consciously focus Repetitively on the learning of the thing. Another key aspect to remember with the Repetition and Compounding Process, is that the subconscious learns by speed. Not by accuracy. So truly, the faster you do the thing you are seeking to program, the faster the subconscious will turn it into a program.

The subconscious is also programmed based on an odd number of the Repetition and Compound Process.

This Principle may be applied in many different ways. One of these ways is sometimes called an "Anchor" or a "Programmed Response." Simply thinking a thought or focusing on a certain feeling or behavior then touching yourself or another person in a certain area such as the shoulder or a finger, then focusing on something completely different (this creates the Compounding), then back focusing on the thought, feeling, or behavior again. Repeat this process an odd number of times and then test the Programmed Response and the thought, feeling, or behavior just comes to conscious.

It's really just that simple. It's the way the subconscious is already being programmed and it's a major part of the process that has created all your conscious thoughts, feelings, and doings already.

Knowing this process of learning so the subconscious just does it without much conscious thought; my daughter was playing the viola and was having a hard time doing one of the songs she was supposed to learn and record for her class. She was getting very frustrated and was practicing playing the song. I asked her to just play the song as fast as she could and then do something else for a minute. Then play the song again on her viola just as fast as she could and then do something else again for a minute. Then play the song a third time, just as fast as she could and then do something else for a minute. Then, just turn the recorder on and play the song at the regular speed and turn that recording of her playing the song into her teacher. She did this process and got an A on the recording of the song.

The subconscious stores and govern our emotions, our desires, and behaviors. Self-image and self-talk are stored and governed in the subconscious mind. All Models, Programs, and Memory is stored in the subconscious mind.

The subconscious takes every micro-bit of Data from the environment and responses from the conscious mind and prior to processing through its patterns of Function, it does what is sometimes called "Reverse Effect" to each micro-bit of Data. In other words, the subconscious takes every sight, sound, texture, temperature, all sensory, and other Data in, and creates a complete Opposite of this Data prior to processing any of the Data coming into it.

This process gives us Choice, even on a subconscious level. Still, conscious must give this Choice, Data permission to be one of the 5, 7, or 9 whole bits of Data coming into conscious from the subconscious to be allowed to come into the subconscious.

Some people end up automatically responding very counter to everything that way, you can hear a thing and just automatically respond completely opposite in about .22 of a second.

Remember the mind works in micro seconds and conscious gets Data every .22 of a second from the subconscious.

The subconscious stores and governs major Models and Programs which make up our Identity, Personality, Emotions, Desires, Behaviors, Self-Image, Self-Talk, Language, Learning, and Functions.

Models and Programs are not made from a single Memory, but from a compilation of Memory, and conscious response. All our Memories are stored in the subconscious and are constantly being processed through adding more Data to already existing Models and Programs. There is always capability to create New Models and Programs by creating new Memory and new conscious response.

Models and Programs never change. Nor do they just disappear or go away, once we have certain subconscious automatic Models and Programs, we have them for the rest of our life. When we create new Models and Programs and use them, we have access to them for the rest of our life. You cannot Change Your Brain Models and Programs However, you have limitless space and ability to constantly create new Models and Programs for the rest of your life. It has been said that Albert Einstein used 10% of his brain. For him, that did leave 90% he never used.

When you work to create a new Model and Program in your subconscious, you might notice that the old Model keeps coming back up, it's just the way it is. It doesn't indicate anything different about you than any other human being. Just keep working to create the new Model, adding new Memory, and taking greater conscious control over your conscious response to the subconscious Data, and the new Model/Program will become larger and more automatic.

If you've ever heard it said that it takes Time to change, remember it also takes an action, event, and condition, or process applied in three different locations of Time to see effective change over a period of Time.

The more Repetition and Compounding, with more odd number of times, and you easily create new Models and Programs which just become automatic subconscious function.

This is the same way you have already been programmed, this is the structure and some of the processes which have created the patterns of your life which you and others have begun to call your Identity, Personality, Emotions, Desires, Behaviors, Self-Image, Self-Talk, language, Learning, Function, and You.

Again, these are just Models and Programs and you are free to create new ones as you choose. It's been your choice all along.

Our Identity and Personality are based upon our Past experiences and the conscious responses to them. These are mainly created from sensory Data from the sense of Sound and Sight. Identity and Personality gives our life meaning. It becomes our reason. These are very important to be able to take charge of finally.

All Data, even in the subconscious is changed, in addition to the Reserve Effect process it goes through. The subconscious has Major and Minor Meta-Programs it processes the Data through. These Major and Minor Meta- Programs may be referred to as Data Compression Programs. In addition to the Meta Data Compression process, the subconscious does a structured, patterned, process for placing all this Data together and creating files for the Data. These so-called files of the Data, end up being our Models and Programs for our Identity, Personality, and everything we just call the self. These Structures, Processes, and Patterns, along with the Major and Minor Meta-Programs all takes place prior to the Conscious having any access to any of this Data. Then again, the same Elements in the brain and throughout the central nervous system repeats this exact same order to add the conscious Functions (conscious being an Element of the brain). It's Function again, being to Perceive, Evaluate, Judge, and Decide about the Data subconscious sent it. Then it all gets added again to the Models and Programs already existing. Or, if you start to take charge yourself, the subconscious will begin to create new Models and Programs. These new Models and Programs will then become new Identity, Personality, Emotion, Desire, Self-Image, Self-talk and you begin to have, on a conscious level, greater, new Choice as to your Identity and whole self.

The subconscious mostly works with Sensory Data, sometimes referred to as Sensory Symbols. This is the reason many techniques or modalities to consciously work with the subconscious, you do not need to know any other Information about anything. All you need to know, for example, is some Sensory Symbols, i.e.: Color and Shape, Sound, Temperature or Texture, Energy, Smell and Taste.

The Subconscious also works with and does the same patterns and processes with Symbols in general. This is in religion, cultural history, science, medicine, and many professional fields and is known in the subconscious, as well.

Symbols are things like numbers, letters, objects, and pictures. Symbols can be anything of a non-verbal reference of something visible or non-visible. Many times, symbols are placed together and have common reference and understanding.

Symbols often times are a sign used in writing, which relate to a particular field to represent operations, quantities, elements, functions, relations, or quality of a thing.

Our life experience is symbolic of our subconscious Models and Programs. Any symbol we notice or identify may represent something in the subconscious mind which has been repressed.

Signs and symbols are compared and processed by the subconscious just as much as sensory data is in the subconscious.

A sign may be a motion or gesture by which a thought is expressed, or a command or wish made known, and the subconscious still processes this data. Linguistics has a symbolic function in which a unit of linguistics designates an object or relation of and has a purely syntactic function. The subconscious processes this the same way.

50% of the Data the subconscious processes is sensory Data. The other 50% is symbols, in various styles.

All this Data is processed the same repetitive way in the subconscious. Models and Programs are created in the subconscious from this Data prior to conscious having any access to the Data. The conscious response to this Data is then also taken back into the subconscious and processed through the same Elements, Function, and Laws. And again, added to or creating new Models and Programs.

You are not your Thoughts, Emotions, and Behaviors. You are a combination of all of these, and these are all subconscious Functions processed through a series of Structure, Patterns, and Processes. The Whole of these, make the Whole of you.

Conscious can override the subconscious. In other words, conscious response to the subconscious Data coming into it at a rate of 5, 7, or 9 whole bits of Data every .22 of a second goes into the subconscious as a command of what the subconscious is to do with this Data.

Getting the conscious to respond any differently is a difficult process, due to the patterns of even conscious thought already repeated over a long period of time.

Knowing the ways, the subconscious and conscious Functions, helps to make taking greater charge of our life much easier.

As it is today, we are just Passenger's taking a ride with the subconscious in control. Deciding what we think, what we hear, and see, deciding the way we feel and the action we will take, and deciding our relationships and even our intuitions. We just ride along with little to no say in our perceptions, judgments, and decision. Our Core Beliefs, our Models and Programs, are created, structured, patterned, and processed below beneath the conscious mind.

Knowing the ways, the brain literally works, it's Elements, and their Functions, and the Laws governing its programming will place you in the driver's seat of your life. You may become your own diagnostics and repair, even upgrade, service technician.

Old Models and Programs do not go away. New Models and Programs can be created at your own choosing just doing the same things the subconscious does by its natural Function.

Chapter 2

OVERCOMING LIFE'S ELEPHANTS

We are born without all the programs running in our conscious and subconscious minds. We came to earth with everything we learned from our prior life deep in our subconscious. Things like mortal memories aren't in there yet. We are just here as babes and everything we will experience hasn't been experienced yet, so it hasn't been experienced, processed, or stored. Linguistic is a primary process or function, which programs our mind. Just the simple words used around us, within us, by us, simple words and phrases program much of us. Things we learn and know, can keep coming up for decades after we have learned and know them. Whether we like their coming up or not it's just part of our processes. If we have learned and know them, still they will keep coming up. What we learn and know is part of our programs.

The subconscious just stores and processes the data based on the conscious repeated responses to the data. Whether conscious has access to the information or not is based on conscious responses. I believe we are Eternal Beings. I believe we have and will live forever. I believe we were intelligent beings as spiritual beings prior to receiving our physical bodies. I believe the knowledge of our life before coming to this earth came with us to this earth in each and every one of us. I believe after this life we will continue to live forever. I believe man will be resurrected because of Jesus Christ. I believe when we are resurrected and continue our eternal progression, we will remember this life's experience. We came with our prior knowledge and progression and will return with the knowledge and progression we gain here.

Memory: is what our program/models are made from and memory consists of different elements working together to create a totality of our programs. With the different elements comprising memory, we are able to create memory just with our own imagination. As we day dream or meditate, as we imagine our life experiences and our potentials, these become a part of our memory and therefore, become a part of our program/models.

There are three different kinds of memory stored in our subconscious.

Real Memory; Memories you have from your experiences. These are sometimes referred to as memories you "Think" that you have. They are referred to as ones you "Think" you had experienced because our experiences are just based on the way that we think they are. Our experiences are individual, and others do not experience the same experiences the same way we experience them.

Vicarious Memory; These come from the things we know about regarding our experiences. Everything we brought into the experiences, Included in the Vicarious Memory are things like Real Dreams, Day Dreams, movies, books and a variety of other Data and feedback from our environment as well as our imaginations.

Genetic Memory; Included in these are experiences included in our DNA. Information on Family lines, family characteristics, physical make up and family line characteristics. Genetic memory only includes the event and not the family member's conscious thoughts about the event.

Real Memory is based on what you "think" you have experienced partly due to the fact that the 5, 7, or 9 whole bits of information is already based on what you already believe anyway. Between the fact that nothing can come into conscious that conscious hasn't already convinced the subconscious that conscious will believe it, the Data is also processed in the subconscious by Major and Minor Meta- Programs which changes the Data for compression purposes and conscious access.

Genetic Memory is an Element of Memory which is very interesting. The scripture refer to "Sins of the parents on the heads of the children". There is a variety of theories and approaches referring to genealogy and character traits as well as physical characteristics passed on the generations.

Have 5, 7, or 9 people say the same thing to you. Even if it isn't exact same wording, just same processed, by you or them. This will just automatically come up shortly there after the 7th or 9th time into your own conscious and you will just do or think. Or if you're lucky, you may wonder. Still, it comes up consistently in your thoughts now. The subconscious is programmed by the repetition (the repeating) of sensory data and the conscious response is important to the programs this data creates. The more the data is repeated, the more memory of the data is processed to create the program with. Program models are not created from a few memories, it takes copious amount of memory for a program to function automatically.

All data and programs models comes under the category of memory, whatever your programs are, you have memories that created the programs. Having the same or similar data continue to come in, only serves to add to the same programs. You have to take charge of the data you are willing to allow to come in, just the simple sensory data creates the programs. If you have thoughts, feelings, and behaviors not beneficial to you, then you have programs created from sensory data memory which was not beneficial to you. You can set your own limitations by removing yourself from environment's and individuals giving you data that feeds your old negative programs.

This is a simple explanation for staying away from friends or family who use drugs or alcohol when you are seeking sobriety. This is not an excuse for eliminating individuals or environments just because they trigger the negative program. If the environment is not giving data directly relating to the program, but only triggering the program, the environment might be needful if you will open up to it. Again, suppose you have a program for anxiety or depression, I am referring to not being around others that are anxious or depressed, I am not referring to people or environments where it is your response of anxiety or depression triggered around them. It is your program, the only thing adding to it is your response and other people and environments of the same program. If you have an anger program, do not go to, nor watch fights, nor boxing, nor other violent events, nor be around others that also display angry behaviors. Again, if it's only that your programs are triggered, but the environment isn't doing your negative program behaviors, it might just be an opportunity for you to work on your program.

As human beings it is very difficult to see our own problems. If we don't see them, then we won't work to change the program. A natural human response is to blame others for our own unhealthy programs. Our programs being triggered as compared to our programs being given more environmental data are very different.

Such as an addict or an alcoholic whose family or friends is confronting them and making attempts to get them to be honest and get help, might trigger the addict/alcoholic to use. This is not adding to the addictive program it is only triggering it. Having the program triggered is an opportunity for the person to choose to create or choose a non-addict program.

The fact is that whatever program/model we have, we also have a complete opposite program already in the subconscious. The other programs must have permission from the conscious to be able to be accessed for conscious use. The opposite program/model is a result of the Reverse Effect Function the subconscious does with all data coming in prior to any of it being processed. The subconscious automatically does Reverse Effect. The Reverse Effect is Processing the information that came in, exactly as it came in, and completely opposite on every piece of information that came in. This is something the subconscious does automatically. Again, this is called Reverse Effect.

2 Nephi 2; 11: "For it must needs be, that there is an opposition in all things. If not so, my first-born in the wilderness, righteousness could not be brought to pass, neither wickedness, neither holiness, nor misery, neither good nor bad. Wherefore, all things must needs be a compound in one;

wherefore if it should be one body it must needs remain as dead, having no life neither death, nor corruption nor incorruption, happiness nor misery, neither sense nor insensibility."

Reverse Effect is a helpful function done by the subconscious, there are great benefits to have the exact opposite of any data coming into the brain. Not only does this give us immediate choice, (depending on which data we have chosen to use) it creates an opposite program/model for every program/model you have. Change then really isn't that hard. What is hard is admitting and accepting that the program/model we use is the problem at all, in the first place. So quickly we blame the environment and others.

There are two things, we know of that stop the subconscious from doing this automatic process of Reverse Effect. One is "Absolute Truths", another is "Absolute Choice". There has to be a consistent pattern of absolute truths, or absolute choice, to get the subconscious to temporarily stop the automatic Reverse Effect long enough to get the next words into the subconscious and not be Reverse Effected by the subconscious process. Example:

There is a pattern of using absolute truths or absolute choice. It consists of a pattern of:

Five Absolute Truths

One Conscious Command

Four Absolute Truths

Two Conscious Commands

Three Absolute Truths

Three Conscious Commands

Two Absolute Truths

Four Conscious Commands

One Absolute Truth

Five Conscious Commands.

Absolute Truths might be a person's name, a direct quote of what they have said, the location, the environment, the date, what is, or just happened.

Conscious Commands generally are of a positive nature of what they may do, think, feel, or have.

Such as, "You are reading these words, words are letters put together in different sequences that have definitions, different letters each make a different sound when pronounced individually, there are allot of words made from the letters of the alphabet and you comprehend many words. Words are put together to create sentences when we write, words can be spoken, written or typed, text and your own ability to comprehend more and more words increases tremendously with greater conscious access. Different people put different words together in different ways, people might understand similar words in different ways and some words may sound like other words, and your abilities to comprehend, gain knowledge and wisdoms from language increases naturally within your own subconscious mind for conscious access. This is written as an example of Truths with Conscious Commands. You know these words and your ability to comprehend, open your mind, apply the information to gain knowledge and become wise increases naturally within you. Throughout the scriptures the words of Christ are excellent patterns of this very structure. Absolute Choice examples are also in the words of Christ: "Could ye not." "If ye choose, ye may…" Using the absolute truth when speaking to others, using Absolute choice when speaking to others helps to open the conscious to greater subconscious data's.

Sometimes we may speak in Truths and Conscious Commands just naturally and your Wisdom increases as your knowledge grows from your application of the information from Data as simple as words, increasing you IQ and lifting you to limitless intelligence.

Words play a large role in our programming. Words, all about them, and the way they get put together to create a sentence. There are a multitude of ways to say the same thing. Just using different words in a sentence, this is actually much of the way we communicate in general. We'll say something to someone, and they say back to us, you're saying this or that. Basically, saying the same thing just using different wording. Oftentimes, people actually end up arguing, even though, they are basically saying the same thing, just using different words. This is where a majority arguing didn't have to be an argument or isn't even worth arguing about.

The Bible makes reference to an original language. The Bible story of the Tower of Babel. The following scriptures are words God said in Genesis Chapter 11: Verse 1: "And the whole earth was of one language, and of one speech". (Then, they built the tower). Verse 6: "Behold the people is one and they have all one language: and this they begin to do: and now nothing will be restrained from them: which they have imagined to do." Verse 7: "Go to, let us go down, and there confound their language, that they may not understand one another's speech."

When we speak, the words we use come directly from the pattern of neuro firings from the subconscious that the subject we are talking about has been programmed to have. We are not consciously thinking in our conscious mind everything of the subject or topic or thing we wish to say and then, consciously picking our words and consciously structuring our sentences into the words to present in our verbal language the thought, idea, concept, that we had in our conscious mind. We just think and speak, and the sentences come out structured together with a word here, another word next, and another word there. Let alone we are not consciously thinking nor controlling where we might sigh, where a tune of a word may be as we speak the word, let alone to consciously control or structure where our breath might be per word as we speak. And there are other aspects of just speaking that is subconsciously neuro fired and just is. These other aspects are things such as body movement, body gesture, even muscle tonality and or twitching. All of these and more different aspects are direct result of programmed neuro firings in the subconscious which happens in micro seconds on a subconscious level. All we do is think a thought, have an idea, have a reaction and response and boom everything else is just there and we say. "Well, that's just me." One of the amazing things about these functions is the sentence I just wrote in quotes, "Well, that's just me."

This sentence as well as all these sentences I am writing here are not structured in my conscious mind word per word sentence per sentence. I know what I'm writing, and I know what I am intending to present, the fact is, I am just writing and just presenting as I neuro-fire. Sure, I'll go back and read this, they call this proof reading, others may read this, and proof read and choose to change some of my words. Still the fact of the matter is, my words just come out, just as my brain neuro fires through the information I am presenting. This lets myself and others who know how to do this identify the neuro firing pattern in my subconscious. Which can then tell myself and others who know how to do this what my neuro patterns are and what I am really feeling and programmed regarding this topic.

The words we use are also taken literally by the subconscious. The subconscious in its neuro firings are just letting the words come in the pattern that they are neurologically fired throughout the brain and the central nervous system and they are also literally from the subconscious. In addition to being literal on a subconscious level there are other aspects of words literally taken in the subconscious and one of these is phonological ambiguities. Words that have the same sound but have more than one meaning, such as: the word son and (sun).

Synapse: the point at which a nervous impulse passes from one neuron to another. To come together in synapsis.

How do you eat an elephant? One bite at a time. We all have elephants in our lives though they be clothed in other than elephant attire.

Examples of personal elephants:

- Financial problems

- Health issues

- Family problems

We often expect that we do it all now and do it well, and then feel overwhelmed at the prospect, and then feel like a failure when we do not complete it as we anticipated. Elephants in our lives are manageable. It is our subconscious programs causing us to feel overwhelmed, and sometimes to a point of panic. The feelings of failure and unnecessary pressure to do it now; all these feelings and thoughts come from program/models created years ago and are operating on auto-pilot in the brain.

Thomas Edison made a light bulb thousands of times before it actually worked. We all have the brain ability to also be genius and we are all able to do anything we can imagine doing. The elephants in our lives can overwhelm and defeat us when we expect that we deal with it in one meal setting. Again, the subconscious mind was programmed in the first place through repetition and compounding, so use your conscious abilities to deal with your life's elephants. 1st) Perceive the elephant, the problem or goal, 2nd) Evaluate the elephant, 3rd) Judge the elephant and 4th) Decide about the elephant. This process when taken charge of by you, consciously becomes a simple and easy process and the elephants is your life begin to diminish.

The human brain has its own nature and natural ways of functioning, educating the conscious as to the nature of the subconscious is crucial in overcoming our human nature, our natural man, our self-limitations and beliefs.

Just perceiving the elephant again is often the most difficult part, the elephant is not someone else's problem, it is yours. Blaming the environment or others just creates more elephants.

1): Perceiving is our ability to attain an awareness and understanding of anything. Any and all things we are able to pick out and take in, to detect, discern, distinguish, and notice, to become clear about the meaning of anything. There are other ways of saying this, still you don't even notice, let alone discern or be clear about anything that isn't already an Automatic- on-going subconscious Program or Model within you already.

Sorry, you are not naturally, Open, nor wise, nor changeable, you are the representations of your own subconscious beliefs with your conscious responses added into them.

The perceiving pattern is quite simply to write down anything you are aware of about the elephant you'd like to deal with. List anything you notice about the elephant, list anything you might understand about the elephant.

Do this in simple terms as to what you hear and see regarding the elephant.

2): Evaluate, the ability to determine or fix the value, significance, worth, or condition of anything by careful appraisal and study. Your ability to assign a degree of value or worth, is another conscious Function though the Data it's getting is still based on pre-programs.

3): Judge, the ability to form an opinion about through careful weighing of evidence and testing of premises. The ability to Guess and Think, to come to a conclusion about anything. "Make up one's own mind."

4): Decide: The ability to make a final choice, to select a course of action, of an infinitive choice. Settle, Rule, Resolve, Fixing the Identity, character, scope or direction of something. Determining to do or not do a thing.

EATING THE ELEPHANT IN YOUR LIFE

1st) Perceiving the elephant; and 2) Evaluate the elephant.

Describe all you see and are aware of about this elephant. After each description place a value of 0 to 10 evaluating the importance of that perception of your elephant.

A. List possible things you see that might be wrong with your view of this elephant.

B. List ideas, reasons and concepts for this elephant.

C. What self-talk do you do about this elephant?

D. List things that might be right about this elephant.

E. Describe the ways you view this elephant in your world view.

F. Describe the ways you view this elephant in your self-view.

G. List ways this elephant might pertain to your past.

H. List the direction this elephant might take your life.

3) Judge the elephant at this point. Now, just review all you have written to this point about your elephant, even if you think of something new or different at this point, Do Not add anything to the prior information. Just considering what you have listed already, just consider the value/worth you have determined about your list.

Taking the Perceive sections information of your elephant make your best guess as to an opinion for each answer you gave. Have your opinions pertain to you not others nor your environment. After your opinion of each one then write your own conclusion of your opinion. Example: List things that might be wrong about the way you see the elephant? (Your answer) Maybe I am making progress. (Your opinion of this answer): I'm too subjective about it. (Then determine a Conclusion, the consequences and outcome of what you decided to be your opinion of this information about your elephant). Write your best guess conclusion of your opinion: Not being open to ways of doing it that could come naturally.

A. From your List of the things that might be wrong about the elephant and give your opinion of each of these and then write your best guess of the outcome and consequences of your opinion of the possible wrongs.

B. From your list of ideas, reasons and concepts of the elephant write your opinion of each idea reason and concept. Then write your best guess conclusion of the outcome and consequences of your opinion of these.

C. From your self-talk about the elephant, write your opinion of the self-talk and then write your best guess as to the conclusion or outcome and consequences of your opinion of the self-talk.

D. From your list of what might be right about the elephant write your opinion now of this list of rights and then write your best guess as to the conclusion or outcome and consequences of your opinion of the right about the elephant.

E. From your list of your world-view of this elephant write your opinion of each world-view and then write your best guess conclusion of outcome and consequences of your opinion.

F. From your list of self-view of the elephant write your opinion of each self-view and then write your best guess conclusion of outcome and consequences of your opinion of these.

G. From your list of what might pertain to your past about this elephant write your opinion now of each item you wrote and then write your best guess of the conclusion or outcome and consequences of your opinion of these.

H. From your list of the direction this elephant might take your life write your opinion of each of your answers and then write your best guess of the conclusion and outcome and consequences of your opinion of each.

4) Decide is the final process of conscious function and your ability to deal with any problem in your life and/or attain any goal or dream in your life. This can become a pattern of new choice and course of action in your life. You are in charge of your life and you are the only one in charge of your life.

Just from your lists of Judgement section where you listed your opinions and best guess conclusions of outcomes and consequences of your opinions, take each opinion and conclusion of outcome consequences and now is your opportunity to determine the final course of action, rules, resolve, define character and direct your action or no action at your choosing about the elephant.

Example: your opinion and conclusion of outcomes and consequences of why you saw the elephant: Others pointed it out and I might be co-dependent. Write a new identity you would prefer to have: Independent. New course of action is to spend 10 minutes 3 times each day to evaluate my experiences. New rules: Listen to others instead of just reacting, set short=term goals weekly. Character traits that could help me do this: Self-confidence, determination.

A. Regarding your opinions and outcomes and consequences of what might be wrong about the elephant write:

New Identity for the wrong about the elephant.

New course of action or course of no action for what might be wrong about the elephant:

New rules to help you do this:

Character traits to help you do this:

Scheduled plan of doing this:

B. Regarding your opinions and outcomes and consequences of these about your ideas reasons and concepts about the elephant:

New identity of ideas, reasons and concepts for the elephant:

New course of action or no action for ideas, reasons and concepts about the elephant.

New rules to help you do this:

Character traits to help you do this:

Scheduled plan of doing this:

C. Regarding your opinion and outcome and consequences of your self-talk about the elephant write:

New identity for your self-talk:

New course of action or no action for your self-talk:

New rules to help you do this for your self-talk:

Character traits to help you do this for your self-talk

Scheduled plan to do this:

D. Regarding your opinion and outcome/consequences of what might be right about the elephant:

Create a new identity for the right about the elephant. Write it:

New course of action or course of no action regarding new identity for what is right:

New rules to attain this new course of new right about the elephant:

Character traits to attain new right about the elephant:

Scheduled plan to attain this:

E. Regarding your opinion and outcomes and consequences of your world-view of this elephant;

Create and write the following:

New identity of your world-view of the elephant:

New course of action or course of no action about your world-view of your new identity:

New rules to attain this new world-view:

Character traits to attain this new world-view:

Scheduled plan to attain this:

F. Regarding your opinion and outcome and consequences of your self-view of the elephant, create and write:

New identity for your self-view of the elephant:

New course of action or course of no action for your new self-view of the elephant:

New rules to help you attain the new self-view of the elephant:

Character traits to help you attain new self-view of elephant:

Schedule plan to attain new self-view of elephant.

G. Regarding your opinion and outcomes and consequences of the elephant as it pertains to your past: Create and write:

New identity of your past as it pertains to the elephant:

New course of action or course of no action as it pertains to your past about the elephant:

New rules to help you attain this about your past:

Character traits to help you attain this as it pertains to your past:

Scheduled plan of doing this:

H. Regarding the direction this elephant might take your life and your opinion and outcomes and consequences: Create and write:

New identity of the direction this elephant might take your life:

New course of action or course of no action to take this new direction:

New rules to help you attain even about your past:

Character traits to help you attain this even about your past:

Schedule plan for doing this:

FORM FOR EATING THE ELEPHANT

Perceive and Evaluate Section of Eating the Elephant

Value/worth_____ A.

Value/worth_____ B.

Value/worth_____ C.

Value/worth_____ D.

Value/worth_____ E.

Value/worth_____ F.

Value/worth_____ G.

Value/worth_____ H.

Judge Section of Eating the Elephant:

A. Opinion:

Consequences:

B. Opinion:

Consequences:

C. Opinion:

Consequences:

D. Opinion:

Consequences:

E. Opinion:

Consequences:

F. Opinion:

Consequences:

G. Opinion:

Consequences:

H. Opinion:

Consequences:

Final Form for Eating the Elephant:

Combine all of your New Identities then New Actions, New Rules, New Character Traits and New Plan.

New Identities: Start each identity statement with an "I am" statement.

New Actions: Start each new action statement with an "I will" statement.

New Rules:

New Character Traits: Start beach new character trait with the word "have".

New Plan: Start each new plan statement with the words "I will".

CHAPTER 3

LIMITING BELIEFS AND OVERCOMING THEM

The words a person uses are a means of diagnosing what might be wrong with a person. The subconscious functions which may not be functioning properly – (mechanics) of how the subconscious works, neuro fire processes, differences between conscious, subconscious and the means of processing. Subconsciously there are copious amounts of data. It's only a matter of getting the information to come to conscious.

Confirmation Bias - we only see what we believe. Have you ever seen an angel? Do you believe in angels? Do you believe that you could see an angel? Do you believe anyone else has ever seen an angel? What are the requirements for seeing an angel? What circumstances must there be to see an angel? The questions can go on and on as the statement, "we only see what we believe" isn't limited to just a belief, such as "in angels", but a gestalt of beliefs within ourselves.

Our own limiting beliefs keep us from attaining our desires and dreams. Are you able to experience miracles in your life? Do you attain things you work to attain? What do you truly believe about your experiencing and attaining? Our beliefs are subconscious program/models that were completed by the time we were eight years old. Our beliefs were created by the environments we lived in and the sensory data in the environments. Our conscious responses even at that time were mimicked by us from those around us. The only way to know our beliefs is to know our personal subconscious responses within our conscious response. We can know whether we do have the belief to experience and attain by whether or not we do experience or attain whatever it is we seek and work for.

Conscious can override the subconscious. Though, if conscious is going to take charge, it can't accept its program models of blaming others, making excuses, and/or denying self-potential.

We are only limited by the program/models we assisted in creating to make our personality, identity, relationships, behaviors, character beliefs, strategy beliefs. Every aspect of our being is operated by subconscious programs. There is no excuse to not over-come the self, and it is no one's fault but our own if we choose to not. Even without this information and knowledge, we know when we say something that isn't true or doesn't feel right to us. We have constant messages from the subconscious part of our brain all the time, even about intuitions. We choose to ignore these and then we continue to allow our natural man (the subconscious) to control the intelligent part of our being. (Conscious).

Communication - 6-9 % verbal - 90% non-verbal. Only 6% of our communications within ourselves and with each other are our verbal communication. The remainder of our ability to communicate with ourselves and others are all the non-verbal ways. The non-verbal includes subconscious functions: breath, tonality, gestures, body position, skin tones, and heart rate and eye movements. Almost every function of our physical being that is a subconscious (non-conscious) function is able to communicate great amounts of information to the self and to others.

Verbal communications includes any sound we make in addition to the words we use to communicate. Our words are important and can help us identify our program/models and practicing reading subconscious communicating can give you limitless knowledge of yourself and others.

The Words in our subconscious aren't stored in just a language area they are stored in our neurology in our beliefs and opinions in different areas.

Our words, naturally coming out tell us our beliefs, our problems, everything and anything we may or may not want to know. As they are neuro-firing out of us, all of the words fit into the different categories that we are aware of today.

The word Just = emphasis, causes the subconscious to hover over the words stated after it is used.

Even = the generalization = core belief. All generalizations indicate core beliefs.

"In the beginning was the word and the word was God."

Words: words are symbols and when spoken their meanings can change based upon the emphasis, tonality and other subconscious programs. Words are ways attempt to communicate with ourselves and others.

Noun; generally, serve as a subject to a verb.

Pronoun; words used as substitutes for nouns or noun phrases.

Synonym; Two or more words of the same language that have the same or nearly the same meaning in some or all senses.

Antonym; A word of the opposite meaning.

Adjective; A word generally used as a modifier of a noun to denote the quality of the thing named.

Adverb; A word typically serving as a modifier of a verb.

Verb: A word that is characteristically the grammatical center of a predicate and expresses an act, occurrence, or mode of being.

Taking words literally, figuratively and symbolically can help you understand your personal use of words and discover the program/models they indicate you have.

Try = Fail. Never Give Up and at the same time, do more than "try", even in your use of the word itself. Work at, determine to and other words change help create new program/models.

BUT=Cancels out what you already said.

YET – pre-supposes that it will.

This and That – This is here, self and now. That is there, other, not now.

Primary questions – What, Why, Who, Which, How, Where, When

Replacing primary questions with words like "about", "regarding"

It = I. Use of the word "it" also indicates a belief and refers to the self.

May vs. Might; MAY gives the subconscious permission. Might indicate possibility and strength.

Will; indicates possibility, anticipation of and power

Still, while, as, and, even though - Weave words

Time tense (did, does, do), (was, will, is)

Do do – I do do that.

Pain = a problem exists.

Pain serves a purpose to let conscious know that there is a problem. 1. first thought. 2. then feelings. 3 the physical.

ANGER from PAIN = thought and feeling – DO TECHNIQUE

Can, Can't = capability. SUBCONSCIOUS lets you know through a program what you are capable of simply by the use of either of these words.

Want, Need, Gotta Have, are Addiction words. – Want, Need, Gotta Have = Addictive Language.

The word want has a subconscious neuro fire to keep us lacking that which we are seeking and indicates a program/model of lack referring to the specific "want" expressed.

"We are spiritual beings having a physical experience, not physical beings seeking a spiritual experience." The foregoing is not our original saying but was originally found on a refrigerator somewhere in Canada with "anonymous" as the author. One important keystone of our program is the premise: "We are spiritual beings". As spiritual beings, we believe we have and will continue to live forever. Additionally, as spiritual beings we already have, within ourselves, all of the answers to the questions which face us today. There is much evidence to indicate that through our sub conscious beliefs and programs, all of the situations we each are faced with today have actually been created by OURSELF.

There are many aspects we will be discussing with respect to existing as spiritual beings, to have lived and continuing to live forever. We will break these categories into what we believe to be very simple topics. First, is the unconscious mind (sub conscious). For years man has wondered about and explored data about the unconscious mind resulting in evidence of the wonder, complexity yet simplicity and multi functions of the unconscious mind. Some information describes facets of the unconscious such as the responsibility of the unconscious to control body functions including the following internal processes:

* Heart Beat	* Digestion	* Speech
* Breath	* Body movement	* Metabolic needs
* Circulatory	* Hair growth	* Eye Movement
* Respiratory	* Skin tone	* Habits
* Emotions		

Speech is an unconscious function for which few of us, as we speak, consciously form each sentence and fashion each with a noun, a pronoun, a verb, and an adverb. Even, so we consciously know when we hear a sentence that has not been properly structured.

Examples of improperly structured sentences and properly structured sentences:

1. We was gone when them guys showed up vs We were gone when they showed up.

2. Over there lots of people gone fishing vs.; A lot of people have gone fishing over there.

We each began the study of grammar in elementary school. We also studied words and their meanings; synonyms and antonyms. Dictionary after dictionary, thesaurus after thesauruses break down the meanings of different words and make available the specific meaning of each word. Whether the dictionary is in English, Spanish, French, or any other language, words have one thing in common; definition. The word may be said in a different way, but the message generally remains the same from country to country.

The thesaurus breaks down words, introducing us to words with similar meanings (synonyms). Whatever reference source is used, one reality remains; words do have significance. In addition, even though we all know that words have import, the specific meaning according to our personal dictionary is based upon our personal unconscious program. Thus, the words that we actually speak and how we speak them are portraying an unconscious purpose. When we look at words as they pertain to the unconscious function and also as they pertain to habits and addictions, we discover that they relate to and are directly tied into the unconscious mind. Therefore, to enhance our self discovery process, we focus our attention on specific words in our vocabulary. We then discuss, discover, and deal with words that are directly related to our addictions and habits.

When we first began to realize the power of our words, and beginning to identify the addiction words, Janey had the following experience:

I went into a local gas and grocery store to buy a pack of cigarettes. Entering the store, I approached the clerk and said: "I'd like to have a pack of Marlboro reds in a box, if you would please." As she reached up to get them, I said, "Oh, just a minute if you would please." She put her hand down. I voiced "I really want a pack of Marlboro reds in a box." She gave me a funny look. I added, "Just a minute please." She appeared to view me quizzically as I said, "I have to have a pack of Marlboro reds in a box." She looked at me for 30 or 45 seconds with a questioning look, and I replied, "I really do, have to have them." She reached up to grab me a pack of Marlboro reds in the box and handed them to me.

Words like want, need, have to have and gotta have; are addictive words. They are words that help us identify the roots to our addictions. We are not talking semantics. We are speaking literally. We are speaking about the unconscious mind and it's unconscious functions such as our breathe, our heart beats, our blood circulating the oxygen through our respiratory system knowing exactly where it needs to be and for what purpose it needs to be there. All of these functions happen unconsciously - even as our speech is unconscious.

All of us have had experiences where we spoke unconsciously, without consciously thinking about it and regretted it later. These are experiences where, when the stressful situation is over and you've already said all the stupid things under stress, you then think of all the intelligent words you could have said had your conscious been in charge during the stressful situation. It is not necessarily bad to say, "I want", "I like," "I need" or "I have to have". That's a normal way of speaking. We are claiming that the things we like to have, want to be, have a need to have, or have to have, are phrases that are directly related to the roots of our addictions. Especially in the human mind as they pertain to the spiritual attributes of our eternal being and thus, to human nature.

Examples of the spiritual abstracts (attributes) are:

* Confidence   * Success   * Patience   * Happiness

* Joy   * Love   * Comfort

The abstracts listed above are intangible, spiritual items and cannot be easily obtained by picking them up at the local store, or out of your kitchen cupboard.

Words want, need, have to have, themselves are as arrows pointing to the specific areas that are the roots of our addictions. These wants, these needs, these gotta' haves, these likes and desires regarding spiritual or human characteristics are things most, if not all, human beings believe that they have a right to. It is commonly believed today that it is appropriate to expect to be loved and to be treated with dignity and respect. To expect is to demand and there is no store you can go to for the purpose of buying love, dignity, and respect, or any other of these human spiritual characteristics. There are no catalogue warehouses which sell these characteristics. These are not tangible things and can not be tangibly obtained. Moreover, they cannot be tangibly taken from us. Additionally, they are not items one can just encounter outside of ourselves.

As an individual wanting, needing, having to have something, we can safely assume that we do not believe that we have what we want. Examples of this are:

* having a full belly from just having eaten a big meal; a person does not want a big meal because they just had one.

* When a person has a glass of water, they are not wanting a glass of water because they now have one.

We do not want what we have. Wanting, needing, having to have, implies a lack. Correspondingly, it implies a desperation, depending on the degree of the like, want, need, or have to have on the continuum of want. The greater the belief regarding the lack or the greater the belief in the desperateness of the need, the greater the need or the addiction. Added into this addiction process are the physical aspects of the cravings. An individual may deposit their needs and desperation into anything they decide to put their needs and desperation's into. The hoax here is because whatever an individual chooses to invest their needs and desperation's into is what that individual is going to receive. Thus, the want, need, gotta' have is answered when we suppose that the confidence, courage, patience, or love will be the receipt from this investment. Consequently, if you desperately need, have to have confidence, you will not receive confidence. We are saying that if you desperately need to have confidence, patience, or any other spiritual characteristic you will experience need and will experience situations that lead you to believe that you have to have them. The need itself, will pull or draw in a greater need, and the needing, having to have will grow and grow within and around you until you may find yourself drowning in the very need.

Wanting, Needing, Having to have, implies a lack. The greater the want, the greater the need, the greater the have to have, the greater the lack, as you perceive the lack. The mere wanting, needing, having to have, is counter intuitive (meaning to seek the opposite of what is expressed, i.e. request patience and experience situations to teach patience). Desperation is counter intuitive as it pertains to the spiritual characteristics of human nature (desperation and spiritual attributes are opposite ends of the continuum). If, indeed we are spiritual beings having a physical experience, rather than physical beings having a spiritual experience. If, indeed confidence, esteem, patience, love, peace, and success cannot be tangible items, but are spiritual, intangible things, then as spiritual beings we already have all of these spiritual intangibles, or characteristics. These characteristics may only be in embryo form, and might not yet even be visible to you, but within you, they are.

These characteristics are within each of us from the beginning, we are born with these characteristics. These spiritual intangibles referred to when asserting that we are all born equally before God in the beginning. In the beginning with God we all have within us the spiritual characteristics such

71

as peace, love patience, confidence, virtue, and charity. These virtues are spiritual characteristics, the intangibles we discussed.

If you have ever held a newborn infant, you have been able to glimpse these spiritual characteristics. You experience the purity and innocence, the virtues in the raw. You sense, as you hold that infant, how this infant seems to originate for your home or arms the message, that the infant is a feeling of love, patience, peace, and joy. We can only give what we posses. Therefore, in order for the infant to emanate the spiritual virtues, the infant brings these spiritual attributes into this world with them. Because each and everyone of us was an infant at one time each and everyone of us was born equal, each were born with these spiritual characteristics. Believing that we lack these characteristics, where have they gone? Have we lost them or are they merely hidden under the fears and self-protective behaviors which often become known as our addictions? These intangibles have not quit, they remain within us. We did not lose them any more than we have lost our spirits and are walking around spiritless. Just as we live as mortals with our spirits within us, so do we still have within us these spiritual characteristics. They have not departed. They are only forgotten or covered over with our mortal experiences, causing us to question and doubt the availability of these spiritual characteristics of ourselves. Our spiritual intangibles have been hidden by our mortal experiences and thereby convincing us that we now are experiencing a lack of our spiritual virtues, which very virtues are vital aspects of us, as eternal beings.

When we experience our perceived lack of a spiritual intangible, rather than focus in great length about the mortal experiences that transports us to our perceived lack, we focus instead on the portion we are the mortal experiences that transported us to our perceived lack, we focus instead on the portion we are yearning for. We assume we are without it, then simply say, "I want to have patience, I want to have peace, I have to have confidence and peace, I have to have confidence to be able to do this, I have to have love, and peace in my life, my home needs joy and harmony. We fail to detect that these attributes remain hidden within us. This masking causes us to believe that we are without. And so, buried underneath these addictive words, is all of our mortal garbage. In verbalizing our lack, we actually have found a very nice way to disguise our mortal garbage. Though the words sound very nice, "I want peace," "I want love," "I want to understand", "I want to have harmony." The truth is that wanting peace implies a lack of peace, wanting to understand or be understood implies a lack of understanding.

Peace is not a commodity you can readily purchase. You cannot buy these spiritual character traits, these Characteristics reside within each one of us. Hence, even though it sounds awesome to hear someone say, "I really want peace", simply wanting any of these things keeps them from occurring in our lives. In fact, the wanting implies a lack. The wanting is the beautiful cover which we have programmed and trained ourselves to deposit on top of our garbage. Wanting something does not bring us the something. Wanting and continuing to want, implies a lack. Continuing to want implies a continued lack of the very thing that we want. Unbeknownst to us, underneath our wanting lies the garbage caused by our mortal experience. The mortal experiences which have somehow convinced our consciousness, our consciousness then convincing our unconsciousness that we no longer have the very characteristic that are ours eternally as spiritual beings.

In and of itself, it is not bad to want, to need, to have to have spiritual characteristics. Here with this information you will be invited to simply listen to yourself and others talk. There upon, identify those spiritual characteristics you unconsciously and perhaps consciously believe you lack. Underneath those lackings, those wantings, those needings, those havings to haves, is the root to your addiction and other negative aspects of your life.

We invite you to initiate the discovery process with us. Observe the mortal experiences convincing you that you do not have the spiritual characteristics. Notice the mortal experiences that have convinced you that somehow, somewhere you have lost wisdom, understanding, patience, faith or hope. We also invite you to unite with us in accepting that you remain a spiritual being, having a physical experience rather than a physical being seeking a spiritual experience.

We are not inviting you to stop wanting, needing, or having to have. In order to stop mentioning these words, we do entreat you to practice replacing these addictive words with different words. We solicit your awareness by simply listening to yourself and the specific words you speak. Especially pay heed to the items of want, need, have to have to be able to accomplish the hopes, the attributes and goals that you believe or hope that you can accomplish in your life.

Keep a note pad, a pen or pencil with you at all times. As you talk, listen to what you say, and to the words people around you say, make notes. When you become aware of what you need, what you have to have that is a spiritual characteristic of your eternal being... write it down and replace the want words with words like: working towards, practicing experiencing, to deal with your perception of lack.

Let's walk through some examples of this. Say, for example, we are discussing your addiction. Ask yourself, "what things do you need the most to assist you to attain your goal?" Make a list of the diversified things that you have the greatest need for in order to favor your goals. Be aware that the old pains, fears, and experiences have affected your perceptions of your spiritual attributes (i.e. love, courage, faith, patience) and are causing you to perceive a lack regarding them. Those perceived needs (I need love is a perception arising from experiences where you focused on actions which depicted "lack" instead of actions experiencing love) are the very things which are covering up the roots of your ability; the wants, needs, and having to have that actually restrain you from having.

You do not have to spend allotting copious amounts of time sifting through all of the mortal garbage that is buried underneath your wants, needs, and have to haves. By releasing wanting, needing, having to have, love, courage, faith, patience, you discover the attributes of love, courage, faith, and patience of an eternal being still residing within you. With this release process, you will have given permission to those attributes to surface within you again. As they surface, they will be revealed to you, arranged just as they were in the beginning of your life on this earth.

Though the process sounds simple - and it is simple - there is more to the story. When you release wanting, needing, having to have, what is left in addition to the spiritual attributes is all the mortal garbage that has been covered up with the nice terms:

Want   Need   Have to have   Gotta' have

The I want peace, I want love, I want harmony.

When we release wanting, needing, having to have, not only is the involved spiritual characteristic free to surface again, so are the memories of those mortal experiences. Therefore, you may now have more extensive memories and you may clearly see, through the releasing of wanting, needing, having to have, that your memories now appear different. You will now perceive those memories through the thoughts that perceive through that spiritual characteristic that you once believed to be lacking or was needed. For example, if you want confidence, have to have confidence, in order to attain your goal and you release the wanting, or needing to have confidence, you will perceive your past experiences here in mortality through the eyes of confidence. Another illustration: if you want, need or have to have, self esteem to reach your goal, when you release wanting, needing or having to have self-esteem to have your goal, self-esteem will be free to surface once again from within where it has been underneath your mortal life's experience. You will now view those memories and/or those experiences through the new perception of self-esteem.

As you prepare yourselves to do this assignment have a notebook and pencil or pen. Write as you listen to yourself speak. Especially note when you hear yourself say, "I want", "I need", "I have to have". Summarize whatever spiritual characteristic the want, need or have to have regarding whatever situation or goal you are discussing. Also write what others want, need, or have to haves that are also spiritual characteristics of man in others as it pertains to whatever situation or goal they are discussing. Once you have made note of these, review these with others. Talk to yourself about them. After they are listed, process each individually. Prepare to release the "want", "need", or "gotta have". Walk through the submodalities of the senses. Symbolize the "wanting", "needing", and the "having to have" through each of the six senses:

Ask the following for each of the senses: "If it had a .... what would it be."

Smell   Energy   Texture   Taste   Color   Sound   Shape

Now release the combined symbols that you have symbolized through the senses. You are releasing the wanting, the needing and having to have. Do not release the spiritual characteristic. Release the wanting, the needing, or the having to have as you have symbolized it through the senses. Do this release by visualizing the combined symbols releasing in all six directions; above, below, left, right, front and back. This is a very simple, yet very powerful way to release "wanting", to release the lacking or the perceived lack of spiritual characteristics.

Another way to deal with the wanting, needing, the having to have, is to go through the sensory based questions regarding the wanting, needing and having to have. Write down the symbols that you have used to symbolize the wanting, needing, and having, to have and your experience with the six directional release process. Now process down the sensory based questions process as they pertain to the wanting, needing and having to have: Where, Who, Why, What, How, Which, When.

There are also words that you can begin to use to replace the words "wanting", "needing" or "having to have". The words we invite you to start to use in place of the addiction words are:

Will   can   may   do   practice   a

We have the spiritual attributes required to face any challenge in our life, the unconscious, being innocent, is responsible to the requirement of focusing on the lack; when we speak the want, the need and gotta have. The belief comes from conscious (via a statement of want, need, gotta have) down to unconscious, stating to unconscious that there is a lack in life in the areas of love, confidence and other spiritual characteristics. Unconscious hears the "lack" and immediately begins to focus on the "lack. Therefore, "I want", "I need", "I have to have...love, patience or other spiritual attributes is perceived by unconscious as a command to focus for conscious on the "want", or "need" and does not judge right from wrong or good from bad. The unconscious does not understand right from wrong or good from bad. The unconscious just is. It only responds as commanded. The process is that simple. The unconscious is that innocent. If the unconscious knew right from wrong as the conscious does, then the functions of the unconscious would be operated from programs differentiating functions based on beliefs of right and wrong. In other words, our breath as an unconscious function would then be evaluated to determine good air from bad air. Based on beliefs regarding good and bad, unconscious would know to cancel breath in bad air, based on the belief that the air was bad, and the body would be harmed by the bad air. It is to the body's benefit, that unconscious does not know good air from bad air and that we can continue to breathe in less than perfect atmospheres. This example shows us that the wisdom involved in programming mortal man so that the autonomic province for the unconscious purpose of breathing is not based upon a program of personal choice as conscious programming is.

Unconscious must have conscious permission to change. It is dependent on Conscious to make appropriate judgement because the Unconscious has not judgement. Hence, it does not know right from wrong. Unconscious is programmed by Conscious and then responds as Conscious has instructed it to do. Would a heart stop beating if it were broken and Unconscious know what Conscious knows about death? Would our heart stop beating, and would we stop breathing if our Unconscious knew the air was bad? Would our heart stop when it was hurt? Seems silly, doesn't it? Language is an unconscious function. We just speak. We open our mouths and words flow. Consciously we know that the words we speak have specific meaning while the process of language is not often a conscious effort. At times, in order to stress a point, we will consciously form sentences together. Sometimes, especially today in the legal world, the meaning of words takes on tremendous importance. In some courts cases, one wrong word can completely change a judicial case. Words have enormous power.

So, too, the words that we speak. They are a literal representation of our life experience. No two people talk exactly alike. No two people structure their sentences in the exact same way. The words we speak in the manner we speak is a matter of personal preference based on the unconscious program we entered into their database of our personal computer; our Unconscious.

Our unconscious programs are based upon our conscious perceptions of our mortal experiences, installed through our senses, based upon our perceptions of life.

Be open-minded, practice the techniques, apply the information to your life and discover what differences occur in your life. Begin, now, for your own benefit, to take conscious control over something that began as a conscious function. We were not born knowing how to speak this human language. We were born knowing how to retain our heart beat, to breathe, to continue blood circulation. Our language, though now an unconscious function, was at one time consciously learned. We were not born with the ability to speak the human language. We learned through lives experience from those around us how to speak the language we speak today, and that life's has meaning, and that very life's today represents a lot of our mortal experience, our mortal perception as we have grown to perceive ourselves, the worlds around us and others around us how we relate to these and inter relate through our life's experience.

Needing   Wanting   Gotta' Have

Practice this technique and write down as you speak what you want, what you need, and what you have to have that are spiritual characteristics. We expect to see you with a note pad and a pen or a pencil as you go through groups/trainings, and through the days and evenings. Anytime, you are interacting, we expect to see you with a note pad and a pen or pencil. We expect to see you writing what you want, need, gotta have, that are spiritual characteristics. You will be expected to share these things in groups/trainings and with your primary counselors/trainer, the things that you have discovered that are your want and your garbage. The symbols that you have chosen, through the sense that you have chosen to describe your wanting, etc. the questioning processes through the senses as they pertain to your wanting, your needing, your having to have. Practice this technique. Begin here and now to take conscious control of that language that we so easily speak. So that those beliefs that are limiting or harmful beliefs, such as I don't deserve peace, I'm not loveable, etc. can begin to change those perceptions by changing your language. Other material with this lesson are the symbolizing through the sense process and the six directional release and the sensory based questions.

ADDICTIVE LANGUAGE

Assuming Conscious Control Of

Our Language

1. TRY – Just TRY. TRY

TRY implies a fear of failure, an expectation to fail.

Demonstration: Fold hands together. Try hard to take your hands apart. Try harder still, and the harder you try, the harder it will be to move your hands apart.

In the word TRY there is the pre-supposition of the expectation to fail.

Replace the word TRY with the words PRACTICE, WORKING AT, DOING

The following words are Addictive Words and imply being without:

1. WANT (Similar words are Desire and Like)

2. NEED

3. GOTTA' HAVE

The unconscious enforces the lacking. Using the above words gives the message to the unconscious to enforce the lacking implied by those words. The "reality periscope" from the unconscious perceives reality and adjusts your perception so that you focus on the lacking and thus, because whatever we put our energy into increases, brings to you increased perception of lacking.

WANT

Release Process

NEED   Symbolize through the 6 senses the want,

GOTTA' HAVE

If it (want, need, gotta have) had a ....what would it be?

Smell   Taste   Color   Texture   Energy

Shape   Name   Sound

WANT, NEED, GOTTA' HAVE

These words appropriate for PHYSICAL NEEDS, such as obtaining a drink or water.

In regard to the spiritual abstracts such as:

Love   Peace   Joy   Patience   Courage   Self-Esteem

Because we are spiritual beings having a physical experience rather than physical beings seeking a spiritual experience, all of the spiritual abstracts are within us........

They may be hidden.

They may be covered over with our debris.

They may endure in embryo form within us.

WITHIN US THEY ARE!

By reason of the effect or message the unconscious receives from us when we use the addiction words, we continually set extend for us our lacking experience.

Words are an unconscious representation of our VALUES, BELIEFS AND HABITS.

Language is an unconscious representation of the total sum of our life experiences.

EXCEPTION: A conscious effort to place words together in a particular structure.

THIS......Here, now (present) closer, associated, focused.

THAT....Over there, past, further away, dis-associated, unfocused.

EXERCISE: Take 3 deep breaths. With the index finger of one hand tap your chest 3 times while saying the word THIS. Notice your personal emotional response. Now repeat this exercise saying the word THAT. Take note of your personal emotional response.

YET............... The Open-Door Policy.

Using the word YET, pre-supposes that the task will be done.

I have not done the dishes........YET.

I have not finished my homework........ implies it may not be completed. Adding the word YET implies that it will be accomplished.

INNOCENCE ------------------IN N O SENSE of child
THE WANTING SELF

CHAPTER 4

BEING LEADS TO HAVING

We are limitless beings. By just using 10% of our brain, we will be genius. The subconscious part of our brain mass will never be able to be exactly duplicated by man. Our conscious thought waves are more powerful than Wi-Fi. The chemical codes of our emotions encode their imprints through our thought waves onto others. We are true, pure energy and as such, will never cease to exist. It is entirely our choice as to what it is that we become, we are not limited by any potential lack. We are only limited by our own self- limiting beliefs.

Man has been partial to his own wisdoms and knowledge since we began life on earth. We are still dependent upon other people's knowledge to guide us.

The potential of the human brain is limitless.

Our materialistic, capitalist culture engenders, promotes, and supports an Identity that essentially lacks; known as the "The Wanna' Self." This is done by its worship of results, its career and job orientation, and its insatiable demand for productivity. Most of America still embraces the Protestant Work Ethic and so have tacitly agreed to the following formula:

DOING LEADS TO BEING LEADS TO HAVING;

Performing or executing actions guides the way and corrects the course for the function of our quality and state of having an existence which guides the way and corrects the course of our maintaining possessions, privilege and entitlements.

This Outside-In Approach to life has indeed brought about lots of satisfaction, success, and prosperity, but is no longer adequate as a success model today.

This Industrial Age formula has been replaced by the Information Age Formula:

BEING LEADS TO DOING LEADS TO HAVING;

The quality or state of having an existence executes action and guides the way correcting the course, performing and executing actions that guides the way correcting the course for function to maintain our possessions, privileges and entitlements.

This is an Inside-Out Approach and yet it is not enough, since it still makes a separation between the Inside and Outside. What is needed is an Integrated Approach that not only links the Inner World with the Outer World but can describe the intimate connections between the two. This is a Whole System Approach, its formula is:

BEING LEADS TO HAVING

The quality or state of existence guides the way, correcting the course as the function to indicate movement or action thereby maintaining possessions, privilege and entitlement.

Notice that Doing is missing. The logical question would be: Who will do what needs to be done? A world cannot function without action; without some part of the system doing something. Stillness, it would seem, results in Nothingness. To understand this apparently impossible approach, it is important to look at the following two premises:

PREMISE #1: YOU ARE THE UNIVERSE

PREMISE #2: THE UNIVERSE IS MADE FOR YOUR SUCCESS

If there is no separation between you and the universe, and it truly is an extension of you and your consciousness, and if it is designed for your success; then just like your thought can make your hands pick up a glass of water, the universe can move in such a way that your dreams and desires are met. In other words, the universe rearranges itself to accommodate your picture of reality. To be more accurate, it would be better to say your "model" of reality.

So, shifting your fundamental model of reality, your world view, results in a shift; a corresponding set of actions by the universe. A flower does very little, it releases a sweet smell that brings the action-oriented bees. Notice that leaders do very little manual labor compared to those who do the hard work in an organization. Traditionally their tasks are more mental, and more recently many experts believe that they have become more spiritual in nature. What type of world-view brings about these spiritual visions of a compelling future?

With which of these three levels do you identify with the most?

- The Metaphysical Foundation involving substance and active forces.
- Universal gravitation (rather than conservation of.)
- Reality beyond what is perceivable by the human senses.

Impressed Force – Force is not an internal property of a single body by which that body determines the (temporal) evolution of its own future state. Force is an action of one body on another essentially distinct by which the first body change is the state of the second body. Fare from expanding the state of motion of a single body, force has nothing at all to do with the state of motion of the body that exerts it. Force expresses a relationship of Real Interaction between two bodies which one body changes the state of motion of the other.

Newton's 3rd law: The equality of action and reaction. Every change of the quality of motion of body is counter balanced by corresponding change in the quantity of change motion of a second body where the first body is the cause of the change of motion of the second body and Visa Versa the 3rd law expresses a (dynamical) community or real interaction of material (substances). (Momentum, or mass multiplied by velocity) Giving meaning to motion itself. True) motions) in a system of interacting (corresponding) bodies are as the center of mass frame of the system which make the 3rd law true.

The significance of the concept of mass is simple to solve by a definition of the concept of true for absolute motion. Apply the law of motion to the observed. Laws of Motion are ultimately grounded in a priori of conditions of possibilities of experience. These facts describe the priori conditions that make objective empirical thinking possible in the first place. (Having unknown short distances between with definite forces running into infinity.) (May appear as opaque constants.)

---Open and Closed Systems; basically, we are not open systems anymore. We are closed systems and our boundaries are not permeable therefore we have no ability to exert any force of our being for success. As closed systems we are imprisoned in our own self-limiting beliefs and will just keep repeating our same failures.

OPEN AND CLOSED SYSTEMS

Humans are by our nature open systems. We are created as open systems. We are ever existing, limitless, potential beings intended to be open systems. Open Systems are entities that are open to feedback with permeable and flexible boundaries. Conversely, closed Systems are not open to feedback and so do not let in new information. Human systems that are closed whether they be individuals, organizations, or societies are addictive systems.

In Nature, success is achieved through Self-Organization. If the natural process of Self-organization is stifled, the system begins to deteriorate. To maintain an upward trend people and organizations resort to methods that force and dominate the system. This takes large amounts of time and energy to accomplish and is ultimately self-defeating.

Once the system is in decline, natural forces come into play, forces whose only purpose is to bring the system to a state of randomness disorder to make the system open.

Conflicting indicators between conscious and subconscious functions happens a lot, conscious can be taught to read the subconscious and identify these.

In a Closed System Anomalies' purpose is to get the system to open back up!

If we are functioning as an open group and someone says something against or opposing, we say thank you, teach us your experience and let us see if there is something, we are missing something we can learn. Recognizing something of ourselves and looking at it.

As we make our statement and ask our questions, we already have our answers within the words that we use.

We are quantum events in the unified field, impulses of intelligence that have learned HOW to create all this universe and there for we as human beings are not self-contained. But in fact, focal points in the Unified Field.

As is the atom, so is the Universe. As is the Human body, the cosmic body.

The subconscious has functions that it does and patterns that it processes its different functions in. The subconscious does not have an ability to do conscious functions. Conscious functions are things like perceiving, evaluating, judging and deciding. Subconscious runs body organs and systems and runs other programs for conscious so conscious does not have to keep track of everything in every given moment. When conscious has perceived, evaluated, judged and decided different experiences in a repeated pattern over a period of time these repetitions become subconscious functions that happen to us in micro seconds. Then we just become the people that we have perceived, evaluated judged and decided to be on a conscious level. These programs work all great and well for us on a conscious level when they work. When they do not work all and well and great for us this is because of subconscious programs neuro-firing as conscious has perceived, evaluated judged and decided that are just not working for us. These are not dysfunctions in the subconscious nor are they other people's problems, nor the wrong time of the day or month or anything else.

For an infant to even have an attitude which is the first consciously recognizable expressions an infant has. Being displayed as a smile or movement of the facial muscles in some way that lets people see an expression of joy or sadness, or some other expression of attitude or experience. These expressions from the infant are indications of human programs being begun in the subconscious about the infant's life experience. In order to have even a slight attitude, it takes about 50 core belief programs in the subconscious. Core belief programs consist of thousands of neuro firings per core belief in the brain and then throughout the rest of the central nervous system. So, one little attitude on a conscious level consists of hundreds of thousands neuro firings on a subconscious level in micro seconds. Then as we grow and learn more such as language, these language words become major parts of these neuro firings throughout our brains and central nervous system. Other sensory experiences, other than words also become and are a major part of our programs and neuro firings, the significance of language is that this is a conscious way that we communicate regularly.

Your mind and body are designed and function in support of you. Your conscious thought create your subconscious programs.

Your Mind consists of your conscious, your subconscious and your creative subconscious.

Your Brain consists of you limbic system, (the Reticular Activating System), Your Brain Waves affect your cellular imprinting.

The brain cannot distinguish between a real experience or one that is vividly, emotionally imagined. The brain adjusts itself to the level of activity which corresponds to the task it is performing. The brain learns habits and patterns through continued reinforcement. In the course of a day we perform many different kinds of acts. Some we do better than others. The ones we do best are those we have learned through established well constituted nerve patterns. (Repetition).

CHAPTER 5

ONLY CONSCIOUS ALTERS

Thinking

Includes self-talk

300-400 words per minutes

Sensory perception

Visual

Auditory

Touch

Smell

Taste

Energy

Self/Time

Conceptual, Abstract concepts.

Emotional, you have a feeling with a thought.

Creative Subconscious maintains sanity by matching your inner picture of reality with the "reality" outside you. As within so without. Look around you and what do you see? You see exactly what is within you. If you do not like the "reality" outside yourself, you must change your "inner picture of reality", and just like magic, "reality" outside of you will change.

Your reality of your world is the reality required to keep you "balanced" based upon your inner reality, your program/models. What you believe in your own programs is what your reality of your world will be. Conscious could be used to a greater degree, even by one considered to be a genius. Conscious can over-ride the subconscious and change the self-view realities. It is able to learn the functions, structures, patterns and processes of the subconscious. Conscious can operate the motherboard of our entire being, changing and controlling our realities as it chooses. Conscious Perceives and perceiving takes action on conscious' part action decides direction. Conscious Evaluates and Judges, these aspects of conscious require zero action from conscious, merely more questioning of the data than what we might usually do. Last but not least conscious Decides, deciding requires allowing others to take action. Simple pattern for helping the conscious functions correspond with subconscious functions. Practice doing this and notice differences in your realities of the world-view and eventually the self-view beliefs and program/models.

Taking greater control consciously of subconscious functions is an incredible way to become a greater being yourself. Being able to recognize your own and others subconscious responses to the world-view reality literally increases your measurable IQ.

I enjoy when people ask what they will be like when they start doing these things, because I get to tell them the truth: "I don't know." I only know that they will start to become their true-self beginning to reach their limitless potential.

The Creative Subconscious takes any given event, experience, or process and creates a past and a future for the event.

Generates drive and energy.

Creatively solves problems.

The Creative Subconscious Maintains sanity by matching your actions to the pictures in the subconscious. Creates drive and energy so if the picture in the subconscious does not match what you now perceive the drive and energy as it creates new pictures are created. It creatively solves problems. Sorting through all the seemingly unrelated information stored in the subconscious for a solution.

The Subconscious mind has its own logic; You Do Not tell it what or how to function!!! You can consciously read it and you can consciously control what programs it runs with your conscious thought, you can even create new programs consciously. But you cannot change the way it is created to function and operate.

The subconscious is the Subjective Mind, meaning it is subject to all data coming in including conscious thoughts. It was discovered as a separate mode of consciousness due to Mesmer's work 1840-1850. It functions as a record keeper of everything literally and does not edit what happened, what you said to yourself about what happened, and how you felt about what happened. It's a memory bank and stores words, pictures, experiences and emotions permanently. It is the builder of the body and maintains automatic functions such as heartbeat, breath, digestion. It may also control time of death. It is the seat of our emotions and our emotions govern the strength of our desires and our desires govern our behaviors. It is the seat of the imagination and creative imagination is one of the greatest secrets of our success. It is the home of self-image our picture of self, repetitive experiences emotions and self-talk. It is the attitudes and beliefs about our self and others. Automatic learning comes from this becomes automatic by repetition such as walking, dancing, typing driving sports.

If you would like to tell the Subconscious the way to operate your programs, then change your programs. Begin by changing your thought.

Some people think in words, words are something we have to learn after birth. Some people think in pictures. Words however are a major way of communication. Words are how we write. Centuries ago pictures were how people wrote, these were called hieroglyphics. The 50 core beliefs that it takes for an infant to have an attitude grows as we grow but they do not become different core beliefs. They become more developed core belief but have the same original neuro fire and same original core belief. When core belief work is done it is always done to the infant stage and core belief work comes out in verbal expressions with simple sentences that we would have said as infants.

Also, the subconscious does not sort any of those experience, perception, interpretation, anything coming into it belongs to. Conscious can and sometimes does. But what is happening on a conscious level, we are consciously aware of while what is happening on a subconscious level, we are not conscious aware of. So, whether infant, toddler, adolescent or adult, conscious has to process what the individual perceives, evaluated judges and decides its processes and the perceptions, evaluations judgments and decisions of the other peoples are the other people's. If conscious does not do this then the subconscious won't either. So, what others perceive, evaluate judge and decide can easily be programmed in the subconscious and come out as the individuals when it isn't theirs at all. Leaving many of us to not know ourselves from others in regard to our perceptions, evaluations, judgments, and decisions. The subconscious is a tool for conscious. The subconscious runs body functions so conscious doesn't have to keep track of heat beat, respiration, circulation, or digestion. And once we repetitively process in a given way our conscious functions of perception evaluation judgment and decision, the subconscious accepts these programs for a conscious function and runs them through its neuro firing, and we just are...

Many words are just based and categorized within our human senses. Based on things we hear, see, smell, taste, feel, and energies we perceive, evaluate, judge and decide about. The sensory neuro firings have general consistent patterns they do in the subconscious in micro seconds. Depending on which human sense is fired first there is a consistent pattern of senses that will automatically fire after the first human sense is fired. These patterns can be inherited, culturally based, and experiential based and are also prevalent regarding other people's patterns when we are quoting or mimicking another human being. There is generally a successful way that the subconscious neuro fires through the sensory information and again depending on the sense first fired, ways the subconscious fires after the first sense fired that does not work well for the individual.

SENSORY FUNCTIONS

Conscious Functions, Processes, Programs:

1: To perceive (5, 7, or 9 items every .22 of a second)

2: Evaluate the perceptions

3: Judge Evaluations

4: Decide based on judgments.

The Human Brain is an incredible machine. It has been studied for centuries. At the same time anyone who looked into the subconscious part of the human brain was considered weird, unusual, as the subconscious was considered dark or evil. Human beings are not dark nor evil nor is the part of their brain that keeps them going dark nor evil. Even though conscious perceives, conscious does not perceive anything that it hasn't already been programmed to perceive. Anything conscious is programmed to perceive is already been perceived by conscious, evaluated and judged by conscious and is either already in a program in the subconscious or floating through our neurology and waiting for more repetitions and compounds to become a program in the subconscious. After having become a program in the subconscious, it then, comes to conscious just as we already consciously programmed it to come from the subconscious. We are not born already programmed. We are born with abilities and certainly DNA has more to do with this than was known before the DNA research. Our conscious perceptions, evaluations judgments, and decisions are based largely on the sensory inputs we have in our environments. The repeated sensory stimuli compounded over a period of time along with the conscious thought regarding the sensory stimuli creates the programs. These programs are not conscious programs. If they were then we would constantly be aware of each program which would make us pretty nuts to have all these running through our conscious minds. These programs stay in our subconscious minds and come up as needed and programmed by our conscious minds.

Punch a key word into your computer for a search on brain functions and you will get millions of hits. A recent research article from a major university in America, where the human brain and central nervous system and limbic systems has been studied for years states that the human brain is the most complicated piece of equipment ever discovered on the earth.

Processes:

Conscious is the part of us that goes through what is known as Altered States, Often times, when the term Alter State is used, people think of the sub conscious. However, it is the conscious mind that goes through Altered States. The subconscious continues in the same state whether we are awake, asleep, or even in a coma. Conscious Alters, not subconscious.

Conscious, in and of itself originated having Alter States.

BETA: is the level where conscious the cycles through its functions at about 14 cycles per second and more. Most activity being cycled every 20-22 cycles per second. If the conscious brain goes above 50 cycles per second, you are in a state of hysteria. Beta is the level we are awake in, doing our regular functions of work, chores and activity.

ALPHA: is the next level of conscious. ALPHA is the same cycles per second that the earth's energy cycles at. Between 7 and 14 cycles per second. Alpha is the state conscious must be in for one to daydream, imagine, or meditate.

THETA: This is between 4 and 7 cycles per second. Conscious must be in this state for an emotion to be recorded to the hypothalamus, (Limbic system). This state to mix the bodies chemicals for the emotion to be recorded or released from the Limbic system. Theta is the level of conscious for a sexual climax.

DELTA: Brain frequencies are less than Theta, below 4 cycles per second. This is considered a state of UN Conscious. Also referred to as Somnambulism.

States of Brain Activity

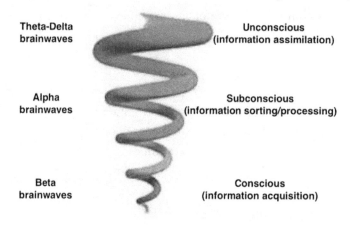

Theta-Delta brainwaves — Unconscious (information assimilation)

Alpha brainwaves — Subconscious (information sorting/processing)

Beta brainwaves — Conscious (information acquisition)

When we sleep, we may cycle through these different states of conscious every 30 to 49 minutes back and forth. A normal sleep pattern may go from Beta, completely awake, to Alpha a bit day dreamy, to Theta, to Delta, a deep sleep state back to Theta, then to Alpha, then even wide awake again and back to sleep again. Different people will acquire different sleep patterns, still the levels of conscious in and out and back and forth are consistent even if the individual's cycling through the different states are very individualized.

When we awake and remember our dreams we have gone from THETA or DELTA to an ALPHA or BETA state. When we have slept even a short time, we have dreamed. Dreams are a result of the subconscious normal functions, TDS. TDS is a trans-derivational search. The central nervous system, a major part of our subconscious, is constantly working, just as does our heart beat, our breath, and other functions. The TDS is the central nervous system firing throughout our body, processing information free floating throughout our central nervous system. This is done always, just as other subconscious body functions are done always, until we no longer have breath, heartbeat, TDS and other subconscious function. The subconscious processes this free-floating information to put it into files it deems appropriate to process the information into. As this process happens, even when we are asleep, the free-floating information is available for conscious access. In order to remember the information being processed (dreams), we have to go from a 4 to 7 cycle (theta) state of conscious or a 4-cycle state of conscious (delta) immediately to a 14-cycle state (beta) per a 7 to 14 cycle state (alpha). If we wake up closer, we do not remember our dreams.

Subconscious functions, processes, programs:

Internal organ functions.

Central and Limbic Nervous systems.

Limbic system records, emotional responses, profanity words, exceptions to mind, body, emotion functions and programs. Limbic system makes these responses function in the body, individual. The hypothalamus is the body's functions brain, muscle movement.

Right hemisphere records options, creative.

Left Hemisphere records Data, routines.

Data, information,

Records everything.

CHAPTER 6

INTELLIGENCE AND BELIEF

For decades film makers have been making movies, even in the days of black and white movies about robots programmed to do things for man. Movies about robots that actually gain intelligence enough to come alive and overtake man. This is not that far of the concept that man already is functioning from. Whatever is in our conscious mind, we are consciously aware of when it is in our conscious minds. Whatever we are not always consciously aware of is not always in our conscious minds. When things we already are aware of comes to our conscious mind it comes from our subconscious mind. This is not that hard of a concept to understand. The subconscious programs that come to conscious were put into the subconscious by conscious. Go and learn a language such as Spanish. You learn the language through repeatedly saying the words and studying the language. You repeat doing this over a period of time (which is the compounding part of the subconscious programming) and after, a period of repetitions and compounds, the words just flow to your conscious mind whenever you need them and maybe even sometimes when you don't necessarily need them. They are not constantly repeated in your conscious mind. Where are they kept? In your subconscious mind. How did they get there? You programmed them to be there so you could speak the foreign language.

We are programmed to think, to feel, and to respond in certain, individualized ways based on the sensory inputs we had in our environment and the conscious thoughts we had about the sensory inputs and then the feelings that developed over a period of time about the sensory inputs and thoughts. This all then became subconscious programs that we have a very difficult time changing when and if we get to a point where we have a certain program that just keeps popping into conscious that we would rather not have.

A person cannot do a thing that they believe they cannot do. I have a friend who was told for years by doctors that he could never quit drinking alcohol. He believed these doctors are right. He has quit for up to four years at a time and then went back to alcohol, remembering that he was told by doctors that he couldn't quit.

A movie with Peter Sellers in it, called Being There, at the end of the movie he walks on the water across a pond. No one ever told him that he couldn't walk on water. I enjoyed the whole movie, but this was my favorite part.

Intelligence is not the things we know.

Intelligence is the ways we have of knowing things.

Intelligence is not just a gift. Intelligence itself is an experience, a journey. Words we use can show and increase our intelligence when the words we use help to open our ways of knowing. All of us already have unlimited information's stored in our brains. Information that has been with us, since before we began, as living human beings. To have access to our information, whether we acquired the information since coming to earth or, if we acquired the information prior to coming to earth, we must have ways of being open to having the information on a conscious level. It is said that there is no such thing as new learning. What we call learning in just remembering. To educate means to draw out not put in.

Things we know and can learn are limitless. Things to know are constantly increasing, as new things are discovered all the time. So, just when you think you know everything about a thing, new things are found about those things as time goes on. Look at medicines, the body, histories, and computers. The key is not the number of things known by an individual, the key is the way the individual has of knowing.

There are many things that can block our paths of knowing. Life experiences can stop us from knowing, or even wanting to know. Life itself is constantly teaching information. Unlimited information is always available in life. To begin, it's as simple as the fact of our not believing "a thing". We cannot learn of anything, we do not believe in, (except perhaps through some very hard knocks). There is as much of a variety of belief as there is a variety of people. Often time's people of similar belief have a tendency to group together, judging people of different belief. Beliefs of ourselves limits our ability to learn. Our own internal self-Identity determines not only our perception and reality, our interests and focus, it blocks even opportunities of learning.

It is known that many of what man calls geniuses had great or wild imaginations. Plato, Aristotle, Einstein, to name a few. One could perceive the prophets of old to have had great imaginations. Talking with God and angels, having visions, dreams, seeing into the future.

Intelligence and Imagination do go hand in hand. Some may say, "I don't imagine". Others may say, "I can't imagine". Still, others may say, or think, "I am not intelligent, and I can't imagine." The King James Bible: Genesis 11; 7 states from God: "Nothing will be restrained from them which they have imagined to do."

There are others in our lives always, sharing their knowledge with us. Our ways of knowing can totally block out the things they may have to teach us. Oftentimes, leaving us with nothing but "the school of hard knocks", to learn the things they offered us. Like when you or another has struggled and struggled to overcome a problem. Depression, anger, whatever the life's problem. You or others have gone to others, of a professional basis, or a support basis. They share their knowledge and experience with you, and you may perceive, believe and learn their knowledge and grow or you choose to not and do not grow from another's experience. If you find your response to others being of an: "I already tried that", "I know all about that", "I don't believe in that", I don't need that" "that doesn't work for me, "I can't do that" basis, you do not know the intelligent way of knowing things. Not that everyone's answers are always the same, still there is much to learn just from each other's experiences. We have to be open to ways of learning to gain knowledge and intelligence.

Many biographies of many famous people begin with their not completing even a secondary education, high school. With their being ridiculed and put down by their colleges that worked or studied in the same field as they. The lady who invented penicillin, Madam Curry. Albert Einstein, had an eighth-grade education and was laughed at by others in his field for years. These people were not considered to have high levels of intelligence, in the beginning. In fact, many people considered to be very intelligent today, as we look back on them, were considered, not intelligent as they began their journey to accomplishing some very incredible things for mankind.

There are numerous things that can stop us from being, seeming, gaining, or even using our intelligence. But usually, these things are not brain capacity nor brain function aspects at all. Most of the things blocking our intelligence is our own beliefs, our attitudes, our perceptions of self and the world.

For example, how can we learn the ways of staying sober, if we're an addict that doesn't believe, care about, nor perceive sobriety as a worthwhile thing? An addict that doesn't believe they can stop doing drugs or alcohol or doesn't believe you are even an addict. These very things in ourselves can and do stop us from learning and knowing the things we have probably already learned but stop ourselves from knowing because of the ways we believe, perceive, and our attitudes.

Attitude is not everything. Attitude sits on and is based on core belief. In fact, a person, infant included, must have a gestalt of beliefs regarding the thing they get an attitude about, before they can have an attitude about a thing. Attitudes are only indicators of belief. Depending upon your or another's attitude, you get a good estimate of some of the gestalt or the belief inside yourself or another. Attitude plays a large role in intelligence.

If the attitude is negative in nature, the way to learning and knowing is not open and the learning and knowing will be blocked and won't happen.

If the belief is of a closed or unbelief nature, the learning and knowing will not happen.

If conscious doesn't, isn't, perceiving the learning and knowledge, it will be there, but conscious won't have access to it yet.

How many things were you told you couldn't do? Whether you told yourself or someone else told you. Positive affirmations are one thing. Constant prayer or encouragement of yourself is even more powerful.

All dysfunctional behaviors occur when one of the three systems or senses shut down or is in over drive.

Negative experiences recorded on Time Line are OK but when the Limbic systems needs information from the Time Line memory the synaptic nerve endings change to jump across to receptors through the memory storage area and all negative chemicals are released into the individual's system from that memory. This memory response is rarely known to have happened by the individual experiencing the response from this neuro firing in the subconscious.

Negative memories tend to get stuck (stored) together because of the common emotional response, (limbic system, chemicals in common), not because of the common event. For example, emotions of loneliness and hunger are almost the exact identical chemical composition therefore emotional experience. So, an experience of being lonely fires into the limbic system and triggers the same chemical response as being hungry. Therefore, we may eat and feel better out of loneliness. And when we are hungry, we may spend time with a friend and the hunger may go away for a while.

Negative emotional responses are four times more prevalent than positive emotional responses. The dictionary list approximately 3500 negative emotions and around 2000 positive emotions.

Memories from your pre-birth to now are your resource files of experiences. If all negatives are in front of self, the negative memory is what will come up first.

Emotions swelling up, one after another is an anxiety attack. Anxiety is a painful or apprehensive uneasiness of mind usually over something impending or anticipated. Anxiety is regarding future. Your subconscious mind is going back searching for the experience, waiting in the future then searching past and find similar emotions and puts it out in front of you again. Anxiety floats on the TDS Time line. If you go to find the causes of anxiety it will go away from where you are looking. If you get closer, it will completely leave, causing you to have no conscious idea of any more anxiety.

Morphogenetic Field

We, as human beings, also sense and communicate in energy:

The Morphogenetic Field is an energy field that surrounds the earth. Our energies are linked with and affect this field.

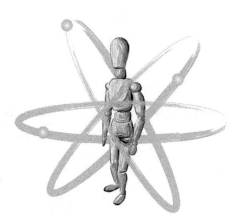

Functions Of The Mind

This course teaches you to identify the conscious, subconscious and limbic system functions. Through this seminar you will learn about automatic programs that run in the background of our minds that greatly affect our lives, the laws which govern and program the subconscious, and ways to learn that the conscious mind may override the subconscious, and change, modify or remove the programs that negatively affect you.

As human beings, we may be described as having three different brains. These parts are so different in function that they may be looked at as separate entities. The three brains consist of:

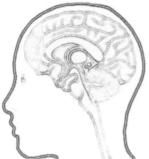

The Conscious

The Subconscious

The Limbic System

The Conscious

The function of the conscious mind is to:

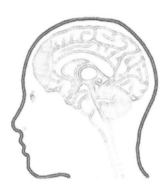

Perceive : to attain awareness or understanding of; to become aware of through the senses.

Evaluate : to determine the significance, worth or condition of usually by careful appraisal and study.

Judge : to form an opinion of through testing of premises.

Decide : to select as a course of action.

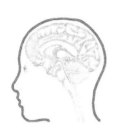

The Conscious

Processes

5, 7, or 9

whole bits of information every .22 of a second.

0.22	1 Sec.	1 Min.	1 Hour	1 Day
5	14	816	48,960	1,175,040
7	19	1,142	68,544	1,645,056
9	24	1,469	88,128	2,115,072

The Conscious

A Whole Bit of
information consists of:

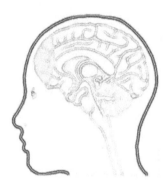

Content : raw data

Context : information that gives data
    meaning

Intent : a direction of action.

Three different decisions are available from
    each whole bit
1. Take Action
2. Let Someone Else Take Action
3. Do Nothing

The Conscious

The state of the
conscious may change
when we:

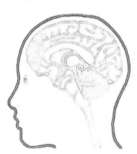

Sleep

Daydream

Watch A Movie

Listen To Music

Take A Math Test

Etc.

The Conscious

These are the <u>conscious</u> states, expressed in Hz, which is cycles per second. (Subconscious and limbic do not change state.)

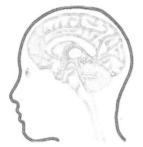

Beta : 13 - 36 Hz

Waking State to Alertness

Alpha : 7 – 13 Hz

Daydream to Relaxed State

Theta : 4 – 7 Hz

Light Sleep to Meditation

Delta : 0 – 4 Hz

Deepest Sleep, considered a state of "unconsciousness."

The Conscious

Law Of Reverse Effect:

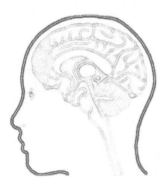

All information processed through the subconscious is processed as it is, and exactly opposite of.

Therefore, information that comes up to the conscious mind may be the original information, or it may be the exact opposite.

The Conscious

Absolute Truth:

Defeats the Law of Reverse effect because absolute truth has no opposite!

Therefore, absolute truth is processed only as is.

After repetition of absolute truth, the conscious may process any information as truth.

Marker Statements use this principle to cause information to be processed as truth.

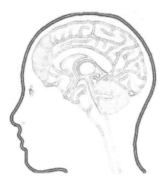

Marker Statements

Statements are read in 5-4-3-2-1 pattern. First say 5 AT, then say 1 DO. Then say 4 AT, and say 2 DO, etc. After practice, you may learn to integrate Marker Statements into your everyday thought and speech.

Absolute Truth:	Say:	Desired Outcome:
1.	5-1	1.
	4-2	
	3-3	
2.	2-4	2.
	1-5	
3.		3.
4.		4.
5.		5.

The Conscious

Our Basic Human
Programming:

Begins at birth, and is mostly completed by the age of 5-8 years of age.

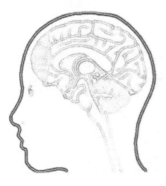

For an infant to show any kind of attitude, at least 50 core beliefs must already be in place to support that behavior.

Possibly millions of core beliefs make up an adult's belief system.

The Conscious

We are born with two
instinctive fears:

Fear of loud noises and fear of falling.

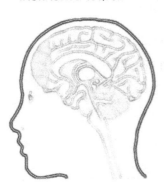

Each of these triggers a startle reflex, which is to flinch, scream, and to throw out the arms and legs.

All other programs are programmed through our own sensory perceptions and consequent decisions.

The Conscious

The Conscious creates programs through:

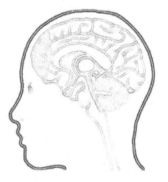

Repetition: Repeating the conscious process over and over. Repetitions of 3, 5, 7, or 9 (odd numbers) are required to create a program.

Compounding: The space between repetition, which causes the conscious focus to shift, and then to program a return to the program again. This down time is essential for any type of programming.

The Conscious

The conscious may override old programs:

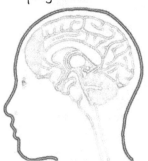

The subconscious runs programs that have been made already by the conscious mind.

The Conscious may always override the subconscious programs. New programs may be made by the conscious repetitively overriding old programs.

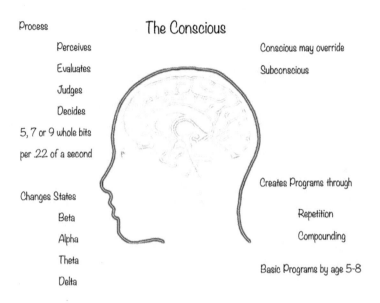

The Conscious

Process

Perceives

Evaluates

Judges

Decides

5, 7 or 9 whole bits

per .22 of a second

Conscious may override

Subconscious

Changes States

Beta

Alpha

Theta

Delta

Creates Programs through

Repetition

Compounding

Basic Programs by age 5-8

The Subconscious

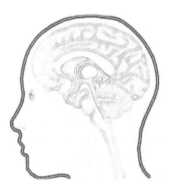

Records And Stores :

All information received through each of the six senses throughout the entire human lifetime, absorbing information on a cell by cell level in the body.

All information processed and programmed through the conscious mind.

The Subconscious

Processes :

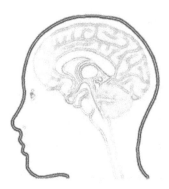

Unlimited micro bits of information per .22 of a second.

(Hundreds of Billions +)

Microbits are simply data. They are not processed, but are recorded and stored by the subconscious.

The Subconscious

Runs Programs created by the conscious mind :

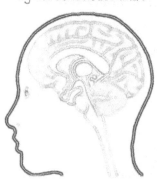

Programs begin in the conscious. When conscious makes a judgment or decision repeatedly, it becomes a program.

Eventually programs run without conscious involvement. Thus they are subconscious programs.

Programs may be as simple as brushing your teeth or as complex as driving a car or texting on a cellphone.

The Subconscious

The Subconscious is programmed by:

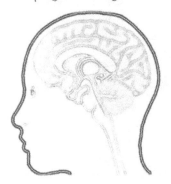

Repetition and Compounding

Speed rather than accuracy

Positive Statements using the "as if" rule

Encoding via Symbols

The Subconscious

Filters information for conscious use:

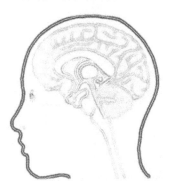

The subconscious filters sensory information in a pattern called a meta program.

Meta programs filter by deleting, distorting or generalizing information by sense. The info then may come up to conscious awareness.

Meta programs themselves may function beyond conscious awareness, however.

Sound		Sight
What?		Why?
Values, Ethics and Meanings		Ideas, Reasons and Concepts
Deletes by Sameness		Deletes by Difference

Touch	Time/ Self When?	Energy
Who?		Which?
Relationships		Intuitions
Distorts by Amplification		Distorts by Diminishing

Taste		Smell
How?		Where?
Beliefs about character		Beliefs about how things work
Generalizes by Sameness		Generalizes by Difference

Human Paradigm Map

The Subconscious

Encodes via symbols :

The subconscious encodes symbolic information through the senses.

Universal Art Symbols :

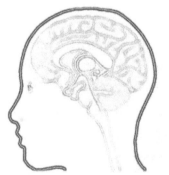

The Subconscious

Does not know the difference:

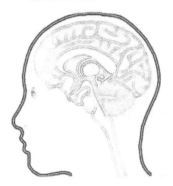

Between Real and Imagined

Between Past, Present or Future Information

All information in the subconscious just IS

The Chemical Brain

The Limbic System

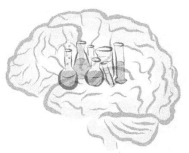

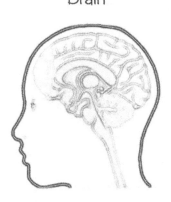

Emotions are chemicals released by the limbic system.

The Limbic System

The Limbic System is subject to the Subconscious :

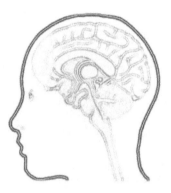

Therefore memories may have stored Limbic System information- such as a memory that causes you to laugh each time you think of it.

Inappropriate Limbic System responses may also be stored, such as a memory that makes you feel unsafe each time you think of it, even though you are safe in the present.

The Limbic System

We are often addicted to our own chemicals:

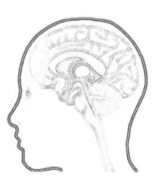

Feelings can be addictive, such as love or excitement. People that sky dive may be addicted to their own brain chemicals, specifically adrenaline.

Some of our own chemicals are responses to other chemicals, such as alcohol or marijuana, which cause the pleasure center in the brain to release dopamine.

Morphine or Heroin have a similar chemical structure to the pleasure chemical dopamine, and therefore stimulate the receptors in the brain designed to link with dopamine.

Memory Creating and Deleting:

What we perceive and experience in our outside world is a reflection of our inner world. Our subconscious programs which consist of: Beliefs of our own and others character traits, strategies and processes of doing things properly, our futures, and many other aspects of ourselves and our world pertaining to beliefs. (Our program/models of our Beliefs create our very Futures, our Behaviors and are the foundation upon all be can become are built upon). Our values and meanings, our ideas and concepts are the foundations of our Identity and Personalities. Our Present moment experiences are all based upon our program/models of our relationships and our intuitions. All of this and the other data in the subconscious is simply processes and stored there as Memory.

Memory created our Past, Memory creates our Present and our Future is already Memory stored in the subconscious. We can take conscious control and create our own Memory, from our Past, Present and our Future. The data is one aspect of the program/model and Memory, the supervising direction of the Beliefs, Values, Ideas, Relationships and Intuitions is the conscious perception of the data. We are in control of our conscious perceptions, even regarding our Past. We have experienced this to some extent in our lives when we have had a negative experience in the Past and later changed our perception of the experience. Doing this can even cause a relief or an awakening, causing us to forgive another or gain compassion. Changing the Past is very important to do when the circumstance of the Past still holds us captive somehow today.

Simple take the negative circumstance of your Past and do a guided imagery of imagining going back to or at least to observing the Past circumstance and observe the experience. As you observe it think of things you might today say to yourself back then to help yourself what you were experiencing.

Again, all these programs/models, beginning as environmental data along with conscious perceptions become Memory and might seem overwhelming. Again, change the conscious perception and the Memory changes with the new perception. Change the Memory's perception and the program/models change: Beliefs, Character Traits, Personality, Identity, Past, Present, Future, Behaviors.

Future is Memory: Data processed and stored in the subconscious and becoming program/models with your own conscious perception. Whatever your perception is may always change, it's under your conscious control you do whatever you choose to do with your perceptions. You have already created your Future and you can change your Future by changing your perception, on your conscious level of your Future. Guided imageries and mediations are very powerful and imagining is processed and stored in the subconscious exactly the same way any other data is processed and stored there. Whatever you imagine your Future to be is what your future may become. If you have a lot of limiting and negative perceptions and program/models of your past, your present and your future, it can take a lot of change of perception to create new program/models. Still, and again, Albert Einstein used 10% of his brain, we all have plenty of brain mass to create new program/models in.

Spend time each day imagining successful experiences in your future, ten minutes each morning and each night may change your life.

When we have a lot a negative memories from our past, we have a tendency to neurologically access them with gestures and movements out in front of us. This also ends up keeping our past in front of us throughout our whole neurology, so any forward movement just makes us feel like we keep going to our past.

Time is an important aspect of our lives: time is an Element of our Reality and the directions we gesture when we speak of our personal time memory experiences can explain much about our life experience. Reality itself consists of Time, Space and Matter. In the subconscious programming change aspects of Time and you can change your Reality. In the subconscious programs Matter is the Data the subconscious uses to create the program/models of Identity, personality, beliefs, behaviors, the conscious perception is a vital part of the Data (Matter) used to create the Reality of the program/models. It can be this simple. Change your conscious perception and you change the subconscious Matter of your Reality.

Oftentimes people think if they change Space, they can change their reality, just move and things will change. Not true, change your time perceptions and functions and change your conscious perceptions of the data coming in from your environment and from your past and future program/models. Change your time directions and conscious perception and change your program/models/.

CHAPTER 7

FIELD OF CONSCIOUSNESS

A field is defined as a region of space characterized by a physical property. Human beings are a physical property and therefore exist within a field. This field is what we call consciousness. Yet there is very little that the average human has been told about their field of consciousness. Analyzing the human being does not identify the field of consciousness. Understanding the way that the human elements function and work together helps to understand the human field of consciousness. Each aspect of being human has its own intelligence. Our internal organs, each living cell, our central nervous system, our chemical systems, our senses, conscious and subconscious is living, with its own intelligence, processes, functions and purpose. The different fields of consciousness work together. They are similar in functions, they correspond together, they are unified together and resonate together and to each other. Each person's conscious field is identifiable and understandable to the trained human being. An individual's level of personal development and even intelligence can be measured and increased just by one's ability to perceive this Field in him/herself and others. This can also be stated by saying that the greater your ability to know your conscious field, the greater access to have to your subconscious knowledge. Conscious field is more than just our thought, our ability of conscious awareness is much more than just thought. It's not just subconscious beliefs limiting our conscious awareness either. In order for one to know anything they must first gain an understanding about the structures, patterns and processes of the human brain and the mind. Knowing this nature of conscious in and of itself will increase your conscious knowing.

The human conscious field is known as the mind field the mind fields consists of three major areas of being human.

KNOW THY SELF

HEAL THY SELF

KNOW AND HEAL OTHERS

Our inner world should not be a mystery. If we are stranger to ourselves, we are just strange. Others cannot learn more of man's wisdom and teach based on man's wisdom about our inner selves. We already know about our inner selves and the mystery is no mystery at all. It's just a matter of accessing ourselves based on our inner workings. There are many things that we know about ourselves and new things are being learned all the time.

There are more things that we know than we can imagine. We came into this state of physical being with knowledge and throughout this existence we have gained great knowledge. You do know so much more than you realize you know. You know for example the number of pine needles on a Christmas tree from the moment you look at the tree. You know the colors and their locations in a painting from the moment you look at the painting. Listening to someone's words, you also hear their tonality, see or imagine seeing their posture and movements as they speak, their facial expressions. All of these and so much more is available to you for conscious knowing. Everything you have ever experienced through your human senses and more is available to you for your conscious to have access to. It is not your subconscious mind stopping you from knowing all things, it is your conscious mind thinking that you can't or that you don't.

121

The more we seek analytical wisdom of others the less we will know of ourselves. Wisdom is not analytical, wisdom itself actually consists of 1st Data received from your environment, 2nd Consciously dialoguing of this Data and conscious theories regarding the Data and 3rd Consciously implementing the theories while continuing to be open to new Data and Dialoging and Theorizing the Data and implementing new theories. Deciding based upon what others have done and why others have done what they did might be some good Data at times to dialogue and theorize about for yourself. Still, the best way to know yourself is to learn to read all of your subconscious aspects and in order to read these you must know what they are.

To know the way the brain and body works, its models, functions, processes is a new self-knowledge of your own models, concepts, and processes. It takes education, implementation, and practice to learn anything, you are in a great position to know yourself because you are yourself. Some people might even get offended when another person tells them why they did a thing or don't do a thing. It isn't the analytical answer that helps us, it is truly knowing each aspects of our conscious and subconscious self. If all of our problems were just in our conscious thought, we might have fewer problems. Our conscious mind can think one thing and the subconscious mind can be doing something completely different. Some examples of this have been when I have spoken with someone and they are telling yes, they understand, yes, they believe what I say while the whole time they are telling me yes, they are shaking their head no. When I explain to them what they are doing, they cannot shake their head yes and speak to me about themselves. Another example is tonality of voice per word spoken. When the voice tone pitch goes higher, the person is actually questioning what they are saying, when the voice tone pitch goes lower it is more affirmed or even like a command.

To know these aspects of subconscious functions to be able to recognize these in our own behaviors and interactions gives us much greater opportunity to knowing ourselves.

The way our eyes move, the words we use to express what we thought we were expressing, the way we gesture, all these different aspects of our being, we may be consciously aware of. Being consciously aware of these aspects of ourselves gives us more conscious awareness of ourselves.

Synergy is the whole greater than the individual parts, this applies to everything. The interactions of two or more agents for a whole. Whatever the whole is, there are three aspects that are individual to the whole. Systems working together are Synergetic. Human beings are whole systems and every aspect of our whole speaks for itself regarding the knowledge it has. Just because you say something, doesn't make it so. Adding every aspect of your whole associated with what you say may well bring what you say into reality. Many people might think a thing yet feel completely opposite to how they think. Others might feel a certain way yet think completely opposite to the way they feel. People can also think and feel a certain way and yet do or act completely opposite to their thoughts and feelings. Many different combinations of this lack of synergy apply to our being human and all are just our individual human experiences and the resulting programs and models created from these experiences. Functioning these ways is not synergetic, these ways of functioning are dysfunctional and drains our energy and diminishes our conscious field.

Systems are enmities or patterns that interact with each other for a process and purpose. The relationship between the parts is the fundamentals of its processing's. If the different parts of any given system are not able to interact openly, inter-dependently, inter-relating with each other the system as a whole becomes dysfunctional. Take a car for a simple example if the different parts with the different systems are not working together properly the car will not run properly. Now, think of an actual human being and the different parts, systems and purposes of the human system. Just the elements of our thought, feeling and behaviors, not interacting properly can put us in a state of panic. Learning to consciously recognize and use your own subconscious functions on a conscious level will help you gain greater conscious control of your entire being.

The conscious field is formed by a unifying force that is intelligent and aware. An individual's level of personal development can be measured by their ability to perceive the field in self and others and the synergy of the whole based on the correspondence and unity of the individual parts together.

When the surrounding plummets, the center collapses, leaving us out of balance, or innocence. In no sense, we don't recognize it nor can we pick up on it in any sense. The surrounding of it, the between, the interactions of the different parts or elements of a whole system. The whole system is the Totality of the different parts or elements such as a Human Being, Time, Reality and any other whole system purpose and synergy.

If mind, emotion and body isn't corresponding properly, the Human Being as a whole plummets. The mind the emotions and the body at an extreme can collapse and the human being becomes completely out of balance and doesn't even recognize it.

With Reality as a whole, when space, time, and matter isn't corresponding properly, our Reality itself plummets and we do not recognize it. If we can't recognize the approximate space with a time or location and the material things within it, Reality is truly unreal.

Reality: Space, time, and matter.

With Time as a whole if the past the present and the future are not corresponding and remember this is inter-relating inter-dependently then Time itself is out of balance and we cannot recognize this.

TIME: Time is a Totality. Measured or measurable periods during which an action, process or condition exists or continues. The Duration of which is a non-spatial continuum that is measured in terms of events which succeed one another from Past, Present, to Future.

Past; Elapsed periods during elapsed events. References to past might be just gone, existed or taken place, in a period before present. This is associated with the sense of Sound and Sight and therefore causes our Values, Meanings, Ideas and Concepts to consciously seem past referenced.

Present; Now and is identified as a division of Past and Future.

Future; Time yet to come, measurements of events yet to be, existing or occurring at a later time.

Consciousness is a shape given form by space and dimension.

Dimension: Height, depth, lateral.

Consciousness is multi-dimensional in our 3-dimensional world and each of the different aspects or elements of our conscious has its own intelligence, function and purpose. These different dimensions of conscious must inter-relate inter-dependently in order for our conscious to be complete as a whole system.

Height intelligence is for values, ethics, meaning, reason, ideas and concepts. The function and purpose is to store our past memories, programs and models.

Depth intelligence is for belief about relationships, relating, actions and intuitions. The function and purpose is to store our present memories, programs and models.

Lateral intelligence is for belief about character, processes, belief about strategies and function. The function and purpose of this is to store our future memories programs and models.

The Human System: The Human System is a Totality. Human system is the whole field, made up of the three other fields working together.

Mind; is Height in the dimension

Emotion (spirit); is Depth in the dimension

Body; is Lateral in the dimension

If these 3 fields of conscious are not inter-relating, inter-dependently and corresponding with their own intelligence, function and purpose we as a conscious being may plummet and not even be aware that we are not truly consciously aware.

The Reality Principle of a system as a whole field made up of three other fields working together: All Realities in our universe are made up of tiny atoms. These atoms though small take up space. These spaces of atoms, matter are called Dimensions.

Holograms are whole and whole systems, one small piece of the whole effects the whole system. This is true in any whole system. Changing one aspect or element of a whole system will change the whole system. Changing the function or purpose of one small aspect or element of a whole system will change the whole system. A whole system, by its very nature is inter-relating, inter-dependently upon each aspect of the whole.

The universe by nature, humans and the human body are Holographic and whole systems. If the different aspects and elements of the universe do not correspond the universe itself would plummet and not even realize it has. Human beings and the human body does plummet often and yet doesn't recognize that it isn't functioning properly.

Human consciousness is holographic as is inner processing and their resulting models, they naturally become whole systems. The natural ability of human consciousness is rarely attained to by most human beings. When someone begins to recognize and remove their programmed limitations to attain some degree of the human nature ability, they are considered genius. When you recognize your own thought, you are capable of recognizing a feeling to go with the thought and recognizing these you have the conscious ability to recognize behaviors to attain the thought. If you have the question, you have the answer. If you have the problem, you have the solution. You do not need to know every single aspect or element of the answer or solution to have it. Just recognizing one small holographic aspect or element will give permission for your whole being to put the answer and solution together for you. You are a whole being, you are holographic, and you are this way by your very nature the key is in corresponding within your whole self. Corresponding consciously regarding the different aspects and elements of your self's whole system.

This is knowledge of the way the conscious and subconscious already works and has worked since Eden. You can take conscious control over your subconscious functions. Knowing the ways your conscious and subconscious work give you conscious choice about the natural man responses. You have experienced this before when you have thought or felt one way and then called someone who has helped you change your thought or feeling or helped yourself somehow.

There is a universal form known as the wholeness model- made up of three elemental levels and one totality level these apply to everything living. Some Totalities or whole system are man-made, and some are God made. There are many totalities I have identified, the list can go on and on, however there are major totalities that effect your ability for be whole beings.

Nature: Nature is a Totality. Nature is the essence, inherent character or basic constitution of a person or thing. Inner force or the sum forces of an individual, controlling force in the universe. Nature is the forces distinguishable by fundamental or essence characteristics. The external world in its entirety and genetically controlled qualities of an organism. Instinct.

Structure; Arranged in a definite pattern or organization, an arrangement of particles or parts in a substance or body. Structure is organized parts as dominated by the general character of a whole system. Structure is the configuration, design and architecture of a whole.

Patterns; Pattern is the natural or man-made configuration of a system with reliable samples of traits, acts, tendencies or other observable characteristics of a system. A system discernable and coherent based on the intended interrelationships of component parts. Structural layout, arrangement, templates of the way a thing is put together, the sequencing.

Processes; Processes are progressive and advancing in a natural phenonium marked by gradual changes that lead toward a particular result. Continual, natural or biological activity or function in a series of actions or operations, conducing to an end. Integrate sensory information received so an action or response is generalized.

Nature will plummet to get us into our patterns and processes. Nature or any given totality will plummet into the center of its elements and aspects, seemingly disappearing. This changes the structure, patterns and processes along with their intelligence, function and purpose. The whole system becomes dysfunctional.

You'll be thrown out of the center of yourself. This is what happens with cancer. You are throwing yourself away and if you don't get back into the center of yourself you will die. Cancer happens as feedback to be a doormat, you can un-choose to be a door mat. When the mind the emotion and the body do not correspond, you plummet inward into yourself. You don't recognize the plummet because you are not taking in feedback, your reality is not real, and your time is not real time. Cancer is just one example of a possible result of this. Cancer also happens on a cellular, so therefore an atom level. The cells themselves are not able to correspond and take in feedback from the other cells and the cells not corresponding, plummet. The whole cellular system becomes dysfunctional we call this cancer. The process of correcting this is to consciously be aware of your own thoughts and the emotions and behaviors associating with them. The interactions between these aspects and elements are crucial to the healing process. Negative, thoughts, emotions and behaviors are indications of dysfunction as do goals and desires that cannot be worked toward.

Anger comes because you have standards and don't want them you want other standards, you want to take other standards and plug them into your own. Anger is a strong feeling or displeasure to a point of antagonism. Standards are rules and principles, conforming to a recognized and permanent value with meaning.

When you become angry is often times when you will lose your conscious ability to even think on a conscious level clearly. Your ability to perceive, evaluate, to judge and to decide is collapsed on by the emotion. You may not even realize that this has happened to you. When the anger has subsided, you can then process whether the rules and principles of another are truly those you would prefer to have. Having standards and beliefs and yet not having the emotions and behaviors backing these is a process again of correspondence between our whole being. When our whole being is not inter-relating, inter-dependently, we become dysfunctional and we don't even recognize our own dysfunction.

The Human System; Mind, Emotion (spirit), and Body

Human system has three basic functions:

Human System is susceptible to or representative of the sympathies and frailties of human nature. As such they interact interdependently in groups forming a united whole. Working together to perform 1 or more vital functions, the body of which is considered as a functioning unit.

Identity, Identity pertains to a sameness of essential character in different instances. Sameness in all that constitutes the whole reality of a thing. Oneness, leaving the multiplicand unchanged. Personal existence of a complex of characteristics that distinguish an individual. The totality of an individual's behaviors, thoughts and emotions.

Communication Verbal or written message through symbols, signs or behaviors. Communication is the exchange of information through techniques of expressing ideas thoughts and feelings.

Creation The act of bringing into existence. Making, inventing, producing, everything that physically exists.

The potential of a whole human being is beyond our actually experiencing yet. To have a oneness of purpose and function to exchange information through various techniques and ideas, thoughts and feelings. The final result being to bring into existence by inventing, producing everything capable of a physical existence.

Because human systems are integrated it is possible to observe human information processing as body movement. Movement equals meaning. This is a major aspect of the field of consciousness and has been researched and studied for centuries. Whether it is the movement of the eyes or body position, movements or gestures. Movement has meaning, regardless of whether your conscious is aware of the meaning of the movement or not. What goes on inside the human brain reflects to the body itself and visa versa. As whole beings every aspect and element of our being is corresponding to system or systems it is associated with.

Nature streamlines systems by having parts or processes at any level that have the same shape or form to resonate together and correspond as one. To have a greater sense of your conscious ability you must first have an understanding of your inner self and their intelligence, function, purpose and nature.

What part of the airplane flies or the car runs? It is the relationship correspondence, unifying, wholeness that lets the airplane fly the car operate and humans function properly.

You are not your senses, your internal organs, your experiences, memories, models, processes. You are the wholeness combined, the entire system totaled.

This is known as Synergy. Synergy is defined as the whole being greater than the sum of its parts.

CHAPTER 8

STRUCTURE OF CONSCIOUSNESS

Humans have three fields of consciousness, these together make the whole human. Each field of consciousness has two senses in it. Each sense has higher level or abstract, conscious functions for conscious use as a whole.

Wisdom: Wisdom is a Totality. Wisdom is the discerning use of knowledge. Being wise indicates that you have an evaluated understanding of an entire system.

Data; is symbols themselves. Words written and spoken, number, sounds, images symbols are ways we transfer Data. Data comes through our filtering systems, based on our perceptions.

Information; the arrangement of Data into meaningful patterns. Math with significant patterns using algebra and geometry. In language, sentences with different chains of words to form patterns for the information. Information is a compilation of our experiences, and theories we create based on our experiences. Others influence this, as well.

Knowledge; the application and productive use of information from data. Knowledge builds models we create from the experiences and theories. Knowledge is the understandings and discernments, beliefs, our whole view of life itself, based on our Data, the Information we took from it.

A key way of attaining greater correspondence and being more Open is to create ways to increase the flow of information throughout the entire system, Communication.

Communicate Continuum: Communicate Continuum is a Totality. This is the process by which information is exchanged between individuals through a common system, as a whole and characterized as a collection, sequence or progression of values or elements varying by minute degrees.

Transmit; Transmit is simply sending or conveying from one to another person, place or thing. Causing to pass on through any medium available.

Receive; Receive is to accept and acquire to be a receptacle. To assimilate through the mind or senses.

Message; Any communication generally of an underlying theme or idea and considered to be the purpose of the communication.

Language Processing: Language Processing is a Totality. Language Processing is words, their pronunciation, and the methods of combining them used and understood by individuals, a group and community. Language is a systemic means of communicating ideas or feelings by the use of conventionalized signs, sounds, gestures, or marks having understood meanings.

Symbolic; Symbols are resemblances to what is referred to, they can represent a whole word or concept. Examples of symbols are ideographic, logographic, and pictographic and often represent learning and even histories.

Energetic; Energetic is an active force, often unseen but can be felt and recognized in other ways. Energy is on an intellectual, emotional and spiritual; level. Fundamental entities of nature can be transferred between parts of a system in the production of physical change within the system and usually regarded as the capacity for accomplishing a thing.

Whole Body; Whole Body language refers to the words, emotions and physical expressions being one together in unison. Complete to the extant that even just the physical body representation might be enough to speak the message without even using words. Whole Body is a full-blown, complete, entire expression of the language.

Message: Message is a Totality. It is the whole of communications of any type. The multiplicand or function governing any interaction between 2 or more individuals.

Intent; This is the meaning, significance intention behind interactions, having the mind, attention, or will concentrated on something or some end or purpose. Intent is what one intends to do, their aim, goal, objective, and design.

Content; The topics or matter of the principal substance, such as written matter, illustrations or music. A part, element or complex of parts.

Context; This is the framework within which something makes sense, the background and frame of references. Interrelated conditions in which something exists or occurs.

As human beings, the information comes into us through our human senses. Human senses are how we experience our lives. From our conscious experience through our human senses, we create models of our world. These models become our thoughts, feeling and behaviors, our beliefs, values, life styles, and circumstances.

There are two basic systems of change we can do:

Incremental change; is making small shifts in different human behaviors or systems. These incremental changes can be endless.

Incremental change:

1. Success patterns exploring possibilities for patterns or systems for change. Exploring to find patterns for success.

2. Extend and improve the patterns and systems for the change. Repeat the pattern over and over again.

3. The system reached its potential and also shows it's built in problems and is not open to new information, data or feedback.

Transformative change; is unpredictable about the way the system will be with transformative change. This is change on an identity level.

Transformative change:

1. Success patterns exploring possibilities for patterns or systems for change.

2. Extend and improve the patterns and systems for change. This is usually a process of repetitions of the success patterns or systems for change.

3. Success patterns considering anomalies (problems built into the system of success from the start. Taking in new information, data and feedback for change). This is where the original success patterns or systems are taking in to anomalies now apparent from the first step of change patterns. Open to feed-back, new data, new information and knowledge. Address anomalies, create new success pattern which addresses the anomalies and go to Step 2 again. Repeat, repeat, repeat, pattern.

Helpless, hopeless, worthless, are key words that the individual is no longer living in their own space, environment, self. There's too much garbage in it to live there. The more we move toward the structure, (space, environment, self) the more effective we are. The more we move away from, deny, refuse and repress the more abstract we become, the less effective we become. So, to just think or talk about a problem doesn't help. We must deal with the model or structures of the problem and we become more effective. Clearing the garbage out of our inner being relieves us from the hopeless, helpless feelings. The garbage we carry inside of us is not always just our own garbage. Many are taught to carry other people's garbage and pretend or become convinced that it is their own. No one is free of having our own problems or garbage, we all have things we regret thinking, feeling or doing. Communicating with our inner being will help to clear these problems up.

Humans as individuals are created to self-organize, to have unity, correspondence, similarities, deviations all within itself. When these do not listen and respond to each other, there is deterioration. This happens on an individual basis as well as in families, communities, countries and the world.

Once the system is in decline, it moves quickly to chaos (disorder). Chaos in physics is a form of disorder that is discontinuous and non linear but not totally random disorder and degeneration.

Stability (order)--------Chaos (disorder)--------Randomness (total disorder) Between stability and chaos and randomness and chaos is what is known as far from equilibrium states. These states accelerate the removal of the limitations imposed on the system. On this light, disorder can be seen as nature's way of obtaining success.

Stability is dysfunctional and indicates a Closed System. Stability here, meaning no "change" to a point of when change begins developing then old patterns and programs to restore any change back to the original condition will appear again for the sake of stability. This occurring to assure there is zero consistency in our ability to change. Whether talking about overcoming a physical illness or a mental or emotional problem, stability to maintain the problems at all cost. Developing behaviors and attitudes to reinforce support for the values we truly know are not true of us.

The Far From Equilibrium State (FELS) is part of the natural forces coming into play to remove these self view limitations. Aspects of ourselves we have learned to deny throughout our life's experience. Strengths we actually do possess but have been convinced and convinced ourselves are not true about us. You can never avoid your own abilities. Happiness and joy will never combine with refusal to recognize the strengths we have inside. We each do have a True Self, this True Self, is our spirit, our spirit is the reason our physical body continues to live. Take our spirit away from our body and the body dies. Deny the strength and knowledge already in our spirit and even our body will fight to get us to admit our True Self and its strengths.

This FELS is a Totality and consists of three separate Elements: Stability, Chaos, Randomness (complete disorder).

The FELS Totality and its Elements will indicate the degree of limitations of Self View.

Self View naturally sympathizes and indulges practices and beliefs (for self) which are different or in conflict with the True Self the spirit self. In other words, unavailable unskilled potential within the Totality of the True Self our strengths, the knowledge we came into this life with. In other words, weaknesses we claim we have which have the potential to become our strengths.

The FELS purpose is to take the World View to the Randomness or complete disorder state at this state the Closed System bursts. Self View becomes World View and we finally perceive the Self as the World view has been attempting to get us to view. This is a function of Detoxing on the human system for someone addicted to substances. This is the physics behind their change in personal behavior, so much of their dysfunctional patterns just seeming to go away after they complete the detox process. The World View becomes quite different and the Self View limitations are temporarily removed.

There are numerous examples of the application of the physics principle between a person's world view and their dysfunctional programs.

Creating the Far from Equilibrium State for a Closed System accelerates the removal of the Self View limitations.

This means that the World View must give the Closed System Data and Feedback to take the Self View to a state of complete Disorder. In this state of complete disorder, the True Self cannot be denied.

We have identified seven human senses and rumor has it that NASA has identified 22 total human senses. We do know that each sense can do each of the other seven senses.

Chi (ki);

1. Body systems matrix

2. Belief integration

3. Addictive systems

The body system matrix is the way our bodies work. Our senses, conscious, subconscious, meta-programs, organs, systems, is the body systems matrix.

Knowing Thy Self, is literally knowing our body's functions and processes, ways we are as individuals. Just knowing these functions, and processes, aids us in change.

Nervous system; Visual

Respiratory system; Auditory

Circulatory system; Tactile

Muscle Skeleton systems; Energetic/Intuition

Reproductive system; Olfactory

Digestive system; Gustatory

Models, processes, beliefs are made from the body system matrix. These are the basis of each person's reality. Shifting a belief shifts our reality.

In order to attain a state of Wholeness or Health, the individual, family, society, must go through the acute stay to get to Health and Wholeness. Once in the Health or Wholeness state again, natural anomalies appear and once again we go through another acute state to deal with the chronic (anomalies) state to return to the Health and Wholeness. Repeat, repeat, repeat. There is no cure for life's problems whether individual or global. There is, however, natural processes, built into each human individual for growth because of life's problems. Whether they belong to us as individuals or to the world. Natural body functions, internal processes and models for overcoming and growing.

Changing to a state of Wholeness does not stop an individual from being able to experience or do the negative thing, it allows for the individual to choose to do the negative thing or to choose to not do the negative thing. In order to choose to not do a thing, there must be a positive thing to choose to do. Choice, is the ultimate purpose, not control.

Each body system is an intended to be an "Open System" and part of the whole system ("Wholeness"), which is the whole system ("Totality"), when all systems are "Open" and "Corresponding" together we have the "Whole" system ("Identity"). When any system is closed, in any area, another body system is plummeted into by the closed system. This is the body system's attempt to get "Wholeness" back. When it plummets into another system, "Identity" is lost. Our inner enemy is our self plummeting us to open our system up. This then becomes the addicted process, "Closed System". When it plummets. It plummets to the "Corresponding" body system as illustrated on the body map. The "Closed System" can also be identified with linguistics, by the word(s) used to describe the problem you or another individual has. Word(s) corresponding with any of the sensory systems, their processes, models, will identify the closed body system.

Unbridgeability is about choices, choice is a quantum leap syndrome. Be willing to let go to be one with self and God and move to goals, nurture self when others are not willing to choose to go with you, they chooses to stay.

Mind, Body, and Emotions (spirit) has two quantum leaps each.

Right and Wrong

God and Self

Life and Death.

Choice of the first three implies choice of the last three leaps. Resistance occurs when the associated Quantum changes (rest of set) not bridgeable. When all Quantum states become bridgeable, Quantum leaps dissolve and Awareness of Unity occurs. The seventh sense, Self and Time, The Great I AM.

Quantum leaps also applied between the third and fourth sensory firings as the details of the ways of dealing with the anomalies showing up in the third sense fired, to be able to continue with the transformative change process. The Transformative change process keeps the senses from closing and keeps Identity growing and progressing successfully.

Know Thy Self

Then

Heal Thy Self

This process must happen before we can truly Know Others then Heal Others. As Jesus said we must first take the rafter out of our own eye before we can take out of another's eye.

An excellent way to truly know yourself is to know your inner self, your subconscious self. If just knowing yourself consciously only, and yet you still can't overcome or attain what your conscious knows, get to know your subconscious self and you could then consciously overcome your problems better, and you may consciously attain your conscious goals. Conscious can override subconscious. First conscious must know the subconscious programs that are running.

CHAPTER 9

TEAMING WITH LIMITLESS POSSIBILITIES

In The Beginning Was The Word.

Teaming With Limitless Possibilities, Of Which You Are One.

Are all realities existing simultaneously? Is there a possibility that all potential exists side by side? Have you ever seen yourself through the eyes of someone else that you have become? Have you looked at yourself through the eyes of the Ultimate Observer? Who are we, where do we come from and where are we going? Why are we here? Well, that is the Ultimate Question isn't it? What is reality? What I thought was unreal, now for me seems in some ways to be more real than what I think to be real. Which seems now more to be unreal. You can't explain it and anybody who gets too lost in trying to explain it is likely to just get lost.

I think the more you look at Quantum Physics the more mysterious and wondrous it becomes.

Quantum Physics very scientifically speaking is a physics of possibilities.

There are Questions. These are addressing Questions of how the world feels to you of whether there's a difference between the way the world feels to us and the way it really is.

Have you ever thought about what thoughts are made of?

I think some of the things we're seeing with the children today is a sign that the culture is in the wrong paradigm and not appreciating the power of thought.

Every age, every generation has it's built in assumptions: That the world is flat, or that the world is round. There are 100's of hidden assumptions in things we take for granted that may or may not be true. Of course, in the vast majority of cases historically, these aren't true. So, presumably in history is any guide much about what we take for granted about the world simply isn't true. But we're locked into these principles without even knowing it oftentimes. That's a paradigm.

Modern materialism, strips people of the need to feel responsibility and often enough so does religion. But I think if you take quantum mechanics seriously enough, it puts the responsibility squarely in your lap. It doesn't give answers that are clear cut and comforting.

It says yes, the world is a very big place, it's very mysterious. I am not going to tell you what the answer is because you're old enough to decide this for yourself. I'm only sharing with you some of my knowledge of the human brain, quantum physics and the Holographic Human Transformation Theory.

Is everyone a mystery? Is everyone an enigma? They most certainly are.

Asking yourself these deeper questions opens up new ways of being in the world, it brings in a breath of fresh air. It makes like more joyful. The real trick to life is not to be in the know but be in the mystery.

Why do we keep creating the same reality? Why do we keep having the same relationships? Why do we keep getting the same job over and over again with the same results? In this infinite sea of possibilities that exist around us, how come we keep recreating the same realities? Isn't it amazing that we have options and potentials that exist but we're unaware of them? Is it possible that we're so conditioned to our daily lives, so conditioned to the way we create our lives that we buy the idea that we have no control at all? We've been conditioned to believe that the external world is more real than the internal world. The physics model of science says just the opposite, it says what's happening within us will create what's happening outside of us.

There's a physical reality that is absolutely rock solid and yet it only comes into existence when it bumps up against some other piece of physical reality. That other piece may be us and of course we're partial to those moments, but it doesn't have to be either. You know it could be just some unintended rock comes flying along and interacts with this mass of stuff and sure enough, it provokes it into a particular state of existence.

There were philosophies in the past that said, "Look, if I kick a rock and I shout, My toe." I feel that, it feels real, it's vivid. And that means that it's reality. But it's still an experience and it's still this person's perception of it being real.

Scientific experiments have shown that if we take a person and hook their brain up to a certain P.I. machine, scan, and computer technology reveal it. Then, ask them to look at a certain object and they watch certain areas of the brain lights up. Then they've asked them to close their eyes and now imagine the same object. When they imagine the same object, it produces the same areas of the brain to light up.

This caused scientists to back up and ask this question. So, who sees then? Does the brain see or do the eyes see? And what is reality? Is reality what we're seeing with our brain, or is reality what we're seeing with our eyes? And the truth is, that the brain does not know the difference between what we see in the environment and what it remembers because the same specific neuro nets are then firing. So, then we have to ask the question, what is reality?

We're bombarded by large amounts of information and it's coming into our bodies and we're processing it, coming in through our sensory organs and it's percolating up and up and at each step we're eliminating information, amplifying it and generalizing it. Finally, what is bubbling up to conscious is the one that's the most self serving. The brain processes 400 billion bits of information a second but we're only aware of 2000 of those bits. Our awareness of those 2000 bits of information is just about the environment, our body and about time.

We're living in a world where all we see is the tip of the iceberg, the classical tip of an immense quantum mechanical iceberg.

If the brain is processing 400 billion bits of information and our conscious is only getting 2000 that means reality happens in the brain all the time. It's receiving that information, yet we haven't integrated it.

The eyes are like the lens. But the tape that really sees is the back of the brain. It's called the visual cortex. It's like a camera and its tape. Did you know that the brain computes what it has the ability to see. A camera is seeing a lot more around than what is here because it has no objection and no judgment, the only movie that plays in the brain is what we have the ability to see. So, is it possible our eyes our camera see more than what our brain has the ability to consciously project?

The way our brain is wired up we only see what we believe is possible. We match patterns that already exist with in ourselves through conditioning.

A story I believe is true is when the native American Indians on the Caribbean islands saw Columbus's ship approaching, they couldn't see them at all. Because it was so unlike anything they had ever seen before, they couldn't see it.

When Columbus landed in the Caribbean shore, the natives were able to see the ships even though they existed prior on the horizon.

The reason they never saw the ship was because they had no knowledge in their brains and no experience that clipper ships existed. So, the shaman starts to notice ripples out in the ocean, but he sees no ship, but he starts to wonder what causes the effect. So, every day he goes out and looks and looks and after a period of time, he's able to see the ships. Once he sees the ships, he tells everybody else that ships exist out there. Because everybody believes in him, they see them also.

We create reality. We're reality producing machines. We create the effects of reality all the time. We always perceive something after reflection in the mirror of meaning.

As far as holodeck or not, it's a question we don't necessarily have a good answer to yet. I think this is a big philosophical question we have to deal with in terms of what science can say about our world, because we are always the observer in science. So, we are still always controlled by what is ultimately coming into the human brain that allows us to see and perceive the things that we do. So, it is conceivable that all of this reality is just a great illusion, that we have no way of really getting outside of to see what really is out there.

Your brain doesn't know the difference between what's taking place out there, and what's taking place in it.

There is no "out there", "out there" is dependent of what's going on in here (our brain).

There actually are choices in the direction of how a life can go, that are contingent upon small levels quantum effects not being washed out.

Let's talk about the subatomic world and then we'll talk about what it's telling us about reality. The subatomic world is totally a fantasy created by mad physicists trying to figure out what the heck is going on when they do these little experiments. By little experiments, I mean big energy in little space, in little pieces of time. It gets pretty misty on that realm of things and so subatomic physics was invented to try to figure that all out. We need a new science down there and it's called quantum physics and it's subject to a whole range of debatable hypothesis, thoughts, feelings, intuitions as to what the heck is really going on. Matter is not what we have long thought it to be. To scientists, matter has always been thought of as sort of the ultimate in that which is static and predictable. Within all the atoms and molecules, all the space within them, the particles take up an insignificant amount of the volume of an atom or molecule, the fundamental particles. The rest of it is a vacuum.

What seems to happen is that particles appear and disappear all the time. So where do they go when they are not here? Do they go into an alternative universe where the people in that universe are asking the same questions, about those particles when they come into our universe? They say, "Where do they go?" There is a great mystery called the mystery of the direction of time. There's a certain sense in which the fundamental laws of physics that we have don't make any interesting, distinctions between past and future. For example, it a puzzle from the stand point of the fundamental laws of physics why we should be able to remember the past and not have the same kind of existence access to the future. It's a puzzle from the stand point of these laws why we should think something like by acting now we can affect the future but not the past. These things that have a different kind of existence access to the past and future that we have a different kind of control by acting now over the future than we do over the past these things are so fundamental to the way we experience the world.

Intelligence is not the things we know.

Intelligence is the ways we have of knowing things.

It is known that many of what man calls geniuses had great or wild imaginations. Plato, Aristotle, Einstein, and many others. One could perceive the prophets of old to have had great imaginations. Talking with God and angels, having visions, dreams, seeing into the future.

Intelligence and Imagination do go hand in hand. Some may say, "I don't imagine", Others may say, "I can't imagine". Still, others may say, or think, "I am not intelligent, and I can't imagine."

The real "eye" is the "I", in Identity. Dendra is created for each other "Identity" you have. The creation of the emotion is the most important thing to understand. Identity being the sameness of essential or generic character in different instances, sameness in all that constitutes the objective reality of a thing. Considered to be distinguishing characteristics of an individual. Individuality is considered to be the relation established by the psychological identification on oneself.

This "relationship" in Identity is personal and individualistic, each human being having a different "relationship" established by the psychological identification of themselves. This "Identity" ends up establishing the way we perceive ourselves and often times limits our ability to grow, develop and become more.

The "eye" being a light-sensitive sensory structure is the image-forming organ of sight, filled with a jellylike substance, is lined with a photosensitive retina. The eye is the faculty of seeing of intellectual or aesthetic perception or appreciation.

All the eye can "see" is what is already a part of your Identity. You can not see what you do not have the Dendra to see. You can not "see" what you don't already have a "relationship" about yourself to "Identify" within or about yourself.

Emotion is created from the Limbic part of our brain from a combination of chemical, the result of the affective aspect of consciousness: Feeling. Feeling being a conscious mental reaction such as anger or fear subjectively experienced strongly and usually directed toward a specific object typically accompanied by psychological and behavioral changes in the body. Emotion is mental states involving such things as pleasure and displeasure rather than intellectual content. This "chemical combination" becomes our "Identity", our "Individuality", our "Intellect", "Perception" and "Appreciation".

The dendrite is the branching protoplasmic processes that conduct impulses toward the body of a neuron, the Dendra is the chemical combination.

The Limbic System is a group of subcortical structures of the brain that are in charge of emotion and motivation. (Consisting of; the hypothalamus, hippocampus and amygdale). This is a part of the central nervous system.

Whenever a thought has chemical combined with it, the chemical being the emotion with the thought, the thought wave is a stronger frequency and actually imprints upon the cells the frequency of the thought wave. This process makes the thought more powerful. Just thought alone is a greater frequency wave than radio, cell phone, or satellite waves. And the fact that the chemical added to the thought makes this more powerful and even causes an imprint upon the cell gives us some idea of the power of our emotions.

Co-dependency is a psychological condition or a relationship where a person is controlled or manipulated by another who is attached with a pathological condition (as an addiction to alcohol or heroin), in short dependence on the needs of or control by another. Codependency is full of guilt. Guilt is full of feeling of blame, culpability, fault, the feeling responsibility for a wrong.

We are human beings and the only thing wrong about this is, we must overcome our being human to become even what we are able to be, here and now.

If we had conscious control over our entire being, we would not be afraid of aspects of life which are not worth being afraid of. We would choose to have character strengths to assist us in dealing with our life's challenges when faced by them.

Blaming ourselves for other people's problems or blaming others for our problems wouldn't be our choice of attribute.

Considering the limitless amount of data in our subconscious and the minute amount of that data coming into conscious. Conscious processing the data in micro-seconds and big bang, there is our identity, personality, beliefs, emotions, behaviors. All the programs that all this time we referred to as the self seems to be in charge of our past, present and our future.

Conscious already has control of our being, even over the subconscious. Learn the ways to the conscious and subconscious work. Take charge of your being. Read and re-read this book. Gain knowledge of the way your brain works and gain limitless wisdoms of your self, learn to heal your self, and learn to heal others.

I would like to offer my gratitude and thanks to Linda J. Dimmick for all her support, patience, and assistance in my being able to write and put this book together.

Linda is a very unique and intelligent woman with the ability to see the difference in any given person or situation. Since having met her, we have incorporated Measures of Affect Theoretically Relative (MATR). Linda has helped others see beyond their standard visions. Anyone knowing Linda, knows her for her dedication and Christ-like love.

Linda has assisted in editing and proof reading my books. She has taught and helped others to understand the concepts. With her medical degree she has shown the correlation of this information and medicine. She has years of experience in natural medicine and herbology.

Linda has been a great support of all of my research and work. I'm not sure where I would be today if it weren't for her.

Thank you, Linda,
Sincerely,
Janey Marvin

Linda Dimmick is a founder of Measures of Affect, a drug and alcohol treatment facility operating since 1993 in Utah. She received her RN. in 1991 and has dedicated her career to mental health and substance abuse treatment. Linda's experience and education also includes Herbology, Holographic Human Theory and N.L.P. With over 24 years of experience her expertise is respected.

For Information about other books, materials, conferences, trainings, or newsletter contact Janey Marvin at thejaneymarvin@gmail.com

ABOUT THE AUTHOR

Janey is a visual individual, she can "See", what is said, she takes words, literally, figuratively, and then symbolically. Doing words this way has given her the advantage of perceiving, evaluating, judging, and deciding from a variety of angles. Her books help you perceive what they are about, she shows you how to apply the knowledge she shares.

CPSIA information can be obtained
at www.ICGtesting.com
Printed in the USA
BVHW051756170323
660665BV00009B/588